A Bird's Eye View Of My Life

Victorious Veronica

Because of the dynamic nature of the Internet, any web addresses or links contained in this book may have changed since publication and may no longer be valid. The views expressed in this work are solely those of the author and do not necessarily reflect the views of the publisher, and the publisher hereby disclaims any responsibility for them.

Edited by: Thanks to Hannah, Renita, Jessie, Swee Eng, Lily and Jingle for the precious time to make this book a reality.

To order additional copies of this book, contact
Toll Free 800 101 2657 (Singapore)
Toll Free 1 800 81 7340 (Malaysia)
orders.singapore@partridgepublishing.com

www.partridgepublishing.com/singapore

Preview

Your book is an honest, uninhibited look at the rough and ragged journey of a cancer survivor. The vivid depictions of lows juxtaposed with hilariously funny takes on a hospital stay post-surgery, make for a story that simply can't be put down! As a fellow cancer survivor, I am greatly encouraged by your positive long-term perspective, which I know can only remain; in spite of medical reports – through a trusting, intimate relationship with the One who gave you life, Jesus Christ. Oozing with easy-to-read personal accounts, diary entries, song lyrics and more, A Bird's Eye View of My Life is a must read for cancer patients, their families, friends, colleagues and anyone who is interested to know the real stories behind the journey of life beyond critical illness.

Hannah Lee
Friend

This book is about a woman's journey through the valleys of struggles, despair and potential defeat that cancer can force a person into. It brings you into the inner world of indomitable trust, faith and the victory that were woven to enable her to soar on eagle's wings. You enter the life of a once active and capable woman reduced to hospital visits, toilet runs, and disappointments. Yet, as you walk with her, your spirit surges as she gives praise to her personal God amidst pain. You appreciate those little "nothing-to-do moments" as Veron enjoys bonuses in baking, sewing and talking to her "friends." Finally, you get a glimpse of how we, "healthy" people make a cancer patient like Veron feel when we throw well-intentioned comments and concern. This book is Veron's miracle journey with God. It is a journey that teaches us to respond to life with eyes of faith.

Jingle Dans Cortes
Friend

Thank you for the privilege to edit your book. I have been immensely blessed by your courage, tenacity and steadfast faith in God. I can feel your emotions as setbacks came in waves almost relentlessly. It is like the waves crashing on the shore, and just when all the backwash is done the next waves come crashing again. You are like one of the stones constantly being polished on the sea shore till the Great Master is satisfied and picked you up to be...... I am sure many will be ministered and many will come to know this Great Saviour of yours. I am amazed at how He chose to delight you along the way. He sprinkled beauty and lifetime events like a wedding and childbirths. Indeed, He is ABBA Father.

Lily Koh
Financial Consultant
Prudential Assurance Company Singapore (Pte) Ltd

V eronica has weaved together her heartfelt and honest journey as a cancer patient filled with hope, fear, joy, disappointment and peace. Truly, this is an account of the ordinary and the extraordinary, told with extraordinary spirit and courage.

Dr. Toh Han Chong
Head and Senior Consultant
Department of Medical Oncology
National Cancer Centre Singapore

I read Veron's book right through in one sitting! I could not put it down because I wanted to know the test results each time she wrote about one that was coming up. I felt the dismay after each disappointing result she wrote about, but unlike my fleeting sentiments, Veron's sense of disappointment was all too real. I admire the way in which she has managed her condition. With dogged determination, undergirded by her deep faith in God, her love for her family and friends, this journal will no doubt bring encouragement and solace to both fellow-sufferers and carers. Thankfully, Veron's story ends with good news. But I have the feeling that even if it didn't, she will continue to exhibit the inner strength and perseverance that can only have its source in God. Keep soaring like the eagle, Veron!

Rev. Rodney Hui
MV Logos Hope

Foreword

I have known *Veron* (her nickname) for many years and in various capacities — as her pastor, boss and lawyer, at different times and milestones in her journey. All along, I can see that she is strong person, with equally strong convictions and principles.

Like all of us, she has had her share of hard knocks in life, but perhaps the biggest "knock" is what this book is about. It is about how she is able to garner all the strength of character to overcome this fearful knock in the guise of cancer. It is a poignant story that will inspire you because it is a story about faith, hope and love; it is also about courage and determination. Above all, you will be touched by the raw humanity of an authentic person who does not pretend to be super-spiritual, but whose love for and trust in God is without pre-conditions. As you walk this journey with her, you will also be filled with joy because you will sense the presence of God in this journey. Joy, as Pierre Teilhard de Chardin (1881 – 1955) noted "is the surest sign of the presence of God."

I commend this first-hand honest account of one who understands what life is truly about. Veron represents exactly what Pastor Chuck Swindoll must have meant when he said, "I am convinced that life is 10% what happens to me and 90% how I react to it." This book is a journal of how she reacted to the fearful news that she has cancer. You will cry with her and laugh with her at the same time. And at the end of this journey, you will be thankful that she chooses to invite you to walk this journey with her.

Dr. William Wan, PhD.
General Secretary
Singapore Kindness Movement

Contents

Introduction

Beyond Cancer

I thought it's time for me to share my journey with people who are going through similar rough times. Let me introduce myself to give you a better picture of me and my background. I am separated, have lived slightly more than half a century and have two grown up daughters, B and N. Both graduated from University of Melbourne, one as a doctor and the other as a physiotherapist. The physiotherapist is still living and working in Melbourne. B returned to her birthplace, Singapore. She moved to Taiwan with her husband for a year.

I worked with a mission organisation (OMA) in Australia until 2008, and graduated at the beginning of 2008 with a Bachelor Degree in Counselling. I then returned to Singapore to discuss my daughter's wedding and to apply to be an Australia Permanent Resident.

On 9th October 2008, I met B and her fiancé S for dinner at the popular Tampines Mall located close to my home. After dinner, while heading to the MRT for home, I felt pain in my tummy. I headed for the nearest public toilet in the shopping mall. I had diarrhoea (at least, that's what I thought), but to my shock, I bled. The whole toilet bowl was covered with fresh blood. It took me a while looking at it before

I realised I was bleeding! After coming out of the toilet, both S and B asked me if I was alright. Shocked and in denial, I told them I was fine and wanted to go home immediately. When I reached home, I went to the toilet and bled again. I thought, "Should I ask B to come and see this before I flush it away?" It took me a long time, but at the end I decided against it; I flushed it all down without telling her. I was hoping that the next day it would all go away and I would be fine. It was not the case. Late at night I went to the toilet again and the same thing happened. This time, I knew it was for real. There was something wrong with me and I needed to seek medical help.

The next day, after B left for work, I went on the internet to "Google", trying to find out more about my symptom. I discovered that I might be in the final stage colon cancer because I bled. So, I took the courage and called B to tell her what had happened. Of course, I was scolded for not taking the symptom seriously, for not informing her immediately when they were with me. Nevertheless, it was sweet of her to make all the necessary arrangements for me to go for a check up at the Accident and Emergency (A & E) section of Changi General Hospital (CGH).

I went to the A & E and was still hoping that it was not serious. The doctor was not happy with what he saw. He arranged for me to have a colonoscopy done the next day.

My life changed from that very day.

The result of the colonoscopy confirmed I had two tumours, one at the upper colon and the other near the rectum. I needed to have a CT scan done, followed by the doctor's review on 14th October, 2008. It was confirmed that I had colorectal cancer but I would only know which stage after the surgery. I also needed to have a biopsy done on my lungs as it seemed that some spots showed on the scan. I was admitted to CGH on Sunday 19th October for a surgery done on the following day.

Things happened too fast from that point. In just eleven days I went through a battery of tests and my first surgery. I did not even have enough time to process my thoughts or to grieve about the disease – not to mention my lost dreams.

My cancer journey began from that abrupt profuse bleeding. This journey is a journey of testing, of faith and of thanksgiving.

One of the most important things that I am really thankful for is that I have a God I believe in and a FAITH in Him that has brought me this far.

I thank God for giving me loved ones and friends from all walks of life who prayed for me and walked this journey with me. They stood by me, encouraged me, cried with me, lent their listening ears to me, and gave all the support that I needed. My heartfelt thanks to each of you!

This book is written because of all the encouragement and support that I continually get. The proceeds from the sale of my book will be channelled to support various ministries.

CHAPTER 1

Testing Times

On the 10th of October 2008, when I saw the doctor, a scan was arranged for the next day (Saturday). Upon arrival and registration at the hospital at ten in the morning, I was sent to the recovery room to change and get ready for the colonoscopy. Then, they wheeled the bed (with me in it, of course) to one of the surgical rooms. I was given the right anaesthetic dosage to make me drowsy but semi-awake. I heard some conversation and I saw on the screen what the doctor was doing to my colon until I slipped into a deep sleep. Upon recovery, B was there with me, and the bad news was delivered to me. They found two tumours growing, a cancerous one at my rectum and another, at the beginning of the colon which they took a sample for a biopsy. I felt disappointment creeping all over me, knowing I was heading for the unknown.

On Monday I went for a CT scan.

A CT scan is like an x-ray except it can capture more than an x-ray can. It combines many x-ray images with the aid of a computer to generate cross-sectional views and, if needed, three-dimensional images of the internal organs and structures of the body. A CT scan is used to define normal and abnormal structures in the body and/or assist in procedures by helping to accurately guide the placement of instruments or treatments. The machine is like a large donut-shaped equipment and it takes x-ray images at many different angles around the body. These images are processed by a computer to produce cross-sectional pictures of the body. In each of these pictures the body is seen as an x-ray "slice" of the body, which is recorded on a film. Imagine the body as a loaf of bread and you are looking at one end of the loaf. As you remove each slice of bread, you can see the entire surface of that slice from the crust to the centre. The body is seen on CT scan slices in a similar fashion from the skin to the central part of the body being examined. When these levels are further "added" together, a three-dimensional picture of an organ or abnormal body structure can be obtained (extract from www.medicinenet.com/cat_scan/article.htm 14th May 2010).

Before the CT scan, I had to drink a cup of contrast liquid. They mixed Rose syrup with the contrast medication and water. After I finished the drink, the nurse inserted a needle into my hand. This needle would be used during the scan, where the contrasting dye flowed through the needle into the blood stream. When all this was done, I was called into the room to lie on this slim longish stainless steel platform with a thin layer of mattress above. There, I had to put my hands above my head and followed instructions to hold my breath when told to during the scan. Just before they started, the contrast dye was connected to the needle that was prepared and I could feel the warmth of it travelling down my blood stream. The platform would move into this donut-shaped machine and there I had to hold my breath. Thankfully, the procedure did not take long.

Things began to unfold. The doctor's review was on Tuesday, 14th October 2008. I was admitted on the next day to do a biopsy of those spots in the lungs and discharged on Thursday.

On the 18th October, I sent an email to all my friends, thanking them for their support and their love, here is an extract from my journal:

"I would like to take this opportunity to thank each and every one of you; the emails and phone calls (even from Melbourne) that I received this whole week were overwhelming. I felt so blessed to have all of you behind me, praying with me, encouraging me at this difficult time. On top of that, I felt so loved by every one of you."

It was the beginning of a rough and stormy journey, wrought with twists and hairpin turns.

"Dad, I know that when you allow such thing to happen, you must have a reason. I will trust that you are my great God, my Provider, my Healer, my Comforter and my ALL"

(12ᵗʰ October 2008)

I had to entrust this journey to Him.

"Stand at the crossroads and look; ask for the ancient paths, ask where the good way is, and walk in it, and you will find rest for your souls."

(Jeremiah 6:16a NIV)

At that point, I still hoped that all of this was nothing but a dream – just a bad dream.

N took leave from work and arrived from Melbourne on the 15ᵗʰ October to be with me for three weeks. On the one hand I was happy to see her, but on the other, I wished this trip was not necessary, as it brought anxiety and lots of uncertainties for her, too. I spent a night in hospital after the biopsy. With mounting procedures and hospital stays, I had another schedule on the 19ᵗʰ of October followed by surgery on the next day. I kept thinking to myself... "I just want to have a good meal before the surgery!" B met me at the hospital and then we went back home to rest. In the evening, we headed to a Japanese restaurant for a sumptuous meal before the surgery.

I had mixed feelings about the surgery. "What will happen with my life and future?" The journey seemed less than encouraging and more of a challenge. But life, itself is full of challenges, isn't it?

The song from *Jeremiah* 17:14 was playing in my head most of the day:

> *"Heal me O Lord, and I'll be healed, save me and I'll be saved, for you are the one I praise."*

So came 19th October, the day of admission. From the 9th when I discovered the bleeding until the 19th; I just followed instructions from the doctor/surgeon as to what to do. There was not much time to process all that was in my mind or my emotions. In those ten days, I was busy sending emails to all my overseas and local friends, pastors, leaders and to places where I did voluntary work. I was just too busy rearranging my plans, schedules and voluntary work. I was requesting prayers and also arranging for prayer updates to be sent by my daughters to key people (appointed) who would distribute them for me. Relatives and friends were told to contact B or N for visitation so that I would have enough time to rest, especially soon after the surgery. I know most people were concerned but once out of the recovery room, all I wanted was to sleep.

I thought I had everything arranged just to see my two girls after the surgery, but I had another shock and disappointment to see a big group of people. I found that I did not have the time to process my thoughts or even my feelings. My life seemed to be standing still! Like a stopwatch, everything seemed to come to a halt. Before I could deal with the shock and disappointment about my disease, I now had to deal with concerned people who could not refrain from visiting. I knew they meant well but I needed rest and time alone. As a recovering patient, not only did I have a low immune resistance to infections, I needed time to digest my new reality and to cope with the change in my life. Although I was grateful for their care and concern which spurred me on, at that time, I hoped that my loved ones and concerned friends could understand that I needed time to be alone.

I have a very good threshold for pain, having experienced two caesareans sections, and one keyhole surgery to remove the gall bladder due to gall stones. So, I thought, "This should be fine, I should be out of hospital in a week's time or less". I was utterly disappointed, for soon after the surgery, at the recovery room, I felt so, so horrible. When they woke me up, and tried to talk to me, all I could say to them was: "Pain, very pain". My body was trembling with pain. The anaesthesia and the morphine did not seem to work at that point in time. At that moment, reality hit me, and hard! In my semi-consciousness state, I remember calling for God to take that excruciating pain away. Hours later, I was transferred to the High Dependency (HD) room. With tubes all over me, it was so painful, especially when I was transferred to another bed. My whole body hurt with every movement, each change in clothes and every change in bed sheet when I messed it up with vomit. It seemed like torture!

I do not remember much of what happened the first few days because of the drowsy and nauseous effect of morphine. I sensed helplessness and hopelessness creep into my mind. I asked many "whys". The first few nights, with pain so unbearable, I could only cry to the Lord. I thought that in this form, life was just so meaningless.

In that quiet but indescribable painful moment, I remembered God and I could only seek Him for pain relief. Medication was slow to take effect and did not seem to work. But my faithful God was there! He let me feel a sense of peace that soothed me to sleep. Whenever I would experience such unbearable pain, I would instinctively look to Him for comfort.

On the first night in the HD room, I woke up with intense pain. In my sleep, the control button for the "call nurse'" and "the morphine release", had slipped beyond my reach. I also wanted to vomit but I could not reach the plastic bag for vomiting. I tried calling the nurse, but obviously they could not hear me, because my voice was inaudible and I was the only patient in that room. Feeling lost, helpless, and with no one to turn to, I called out to Him. I threw up and messed up the bed, but I still managed to sleep. I am not sure how much later it was when the nurse came to check on me and saw the mess. They cleaned me up and put back all the controls accessible to my reach again. Thanks to God that He is always there.

I was discharged from the hospital on 28th October 2008. At the post-op review, I was told that sixty percent of my colon had been removed. I am thankful that the surgeon managed to join back the colon to the rectum. There was no need to have a colostomy, which involved wearing a special bag to collect the body wastes. The biopsy showed that I was in the 4th stage of colorectal cancer, because it had also spread to my lungs. Though I was thankful for life, I felt I was falling into this deep valley and did not know how to climb up the cliff side again.

As a result of the shortened colon, my body needed time to adjust its function of absorbing liquid. In the meantime, I had to learn to cope with frequent diarrhoea which made me rush to the toilet more than six times a day. Pain combined with speed was a challenge. I had to get to the toilet fast otherwise I would miss it and make a mess. It was difficult to cope – mentally, emotionally and physically. I felt so exhausted. I had landed in the valley.

> *"Thank You God that in my pain, I still can call for You and in my darkest valley, You lead me. Thank You for always being there and that You have never forsaken me."*
> (From my journal on 30th October)

The Scripture for that day was:

> *"Blessed are all who take refuge in Him."*
> (Psalm 2:12b NIV)

Before this cancer journey, I was an active person. My day was packed with programmes and I was completely independent. I hardly fell sick, and thus I felt life was unfair. Why should someone who was strong and healthy have to go through this? I did not understand. Just when I had graduated and thought I would be able to serve in the community to counsel the broken, I was on the standstill in life, not knowing what my own future would be. Reality hit me hard. I had cancer and what more, at 'stage 4'! Then I asked, "What is next? How am I going to walk this journey? How can I pass my day doing nothing? I am not the type of person who can live a day without doing anything! So what should I do?" I had to ask for the next road sign on my journey.

Here is a brief summary of what had happened so far:

- 9th October evening, the turmoil began (the start of bleeding)
- 10th Oct, went for check up
- 11th Oct, went for colonoscopy
- 13th Oct, doctor's review
- 15th Oct, admission to hospital for lung biopsy, N arrived from Melbourne in the morning. What a touching moment at the "A & E" department where we met.
- 16th Oct, due to a little leakage of air, I was kept another night in the hospital for observation
- 17th Oct, discharged from hospital and the rest of the two days spent the time eating whatever I wanted before the fasting on Sunday. It was also time to spend with my children.
- 19th Oct, only clear liquid for breakfast and lunch (lunch would be the last meal before preparation for the operation).
- 19th Oct, admission to hospital again in the afternoon.
- 20th Oct, scheduled for operation at 3:00 p.m.
- 20th – 28th Oct, recovery in hospital. It was hard to cope with pain when there were tubes, bags hanging all over me.
- 28th Oct, discharged from hospital around 3:00 p.m.
- 29th Oct, adjusting back to daily life, trying to walk further, going to the toilet less (hoping it would get less each day), eating more and less pain.

Road Sign on My Journey

I spent nine days in hospital. Being able to have all the tubes removed and to return "home" gave me some mixed feelings.

Since my separation from my ex-husband, I spent most of my time in Melbourne. Whenever I was in Singapore, I stayed with my brother. B and my ex-husband still lived in my marital home. B and N felt that it would be more convenient for them to look after me, if I came back to the marital home after surgery rather than stay with my brother. I chose to return to my marital home on condition that my ex-husband would gave me the space, and that he would not interfere with my being there. This was not an easy choice, for I had to live under the same roof with my ex-husband while we lead separate individual lives. It was going to be a tough journey in all aspects.

After six days being at home, I managed to board public bus to go to church on Sunday. Being able to go to church on my own was fantastic. Although I still had to walk very slowly, I was thankful for every accomplishment on the road to recovery.

Daily Routine

Waking up in the morning, taking the medicine and eating breakfast – they were great accomplishments. But the rest of the day was unpredictable. Just like the Sunday I used the toilet twelve times in all, including a number of times during church service.

Of course, I did have good days, days where I could spend quiet time reading, cooking my own meals and even baking. My problem was adjusting to a slower pace of life.

Emotion

I felt emotionally tired, although the doctors told me that I would be fine after the chemotherapy. I was told that I would experience fewer side effects with the new drugs and that after six months, I should be cleared. But my confidence slowly slipped away as one bad news after another was slapped on me with every trip to the consultation room.

There were times when I did not feel like talking or seeing any friends. I wanted my space and my time to be alone. I longed to be with God, to sort out my grief, loss, and to come to terms with the situation that was changing my whole life.

Food

Though the surgeon said I could eat anything except less fibre, I was still trying to adjust to my food intake as some food would cost me to race to the toilet four or five times a day!

Wound

Even though 37 staples were removed from my wound, I experienced pain at the site of the wound. There was a small area that still needed dressing and time to heal. Although I tried to avoid taking them, I was still on painkiller which I took my maximum dosage just to get through the night.

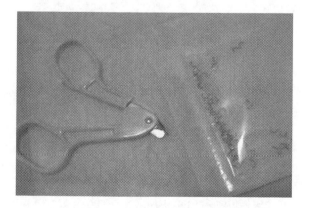

These are the staples that hold the wound together,
and the special scissors to remove them.

Sleep

I thank God that I could sleep much better over the last three nights from discharge. Although I woke up at 5:00 a.m., with sleep disturbances such as nightmares, tummy aches and frequent visits to the toilet, I still considered it the best sleep since the surgery.

Waiting for ...

On the 13th of November, I went for the PET scan which would help to pick up all the active cancer cells in my body. The doctors hoped to know how far the cells had migrated, in addition to the three spots they detected in my lungs. The doctors needed to know if there were any other affected areas. I was praying that they would find nothing, not even the three spots (a little wishful!). The next day, would be the review with the surgeon, Dr. W. This was just a routine check after surgery. I was hoping that he could give me the clearance to fly back to Melbourne before I start my chemo. I desired to go back to Melbourne for inner healing, extended prayer time and to sort out things at my Melbourne home.

I asked my oncologist, Dr. T, if I really needed to go through chemotherapy, and if I could make a trip back to Melbourne for closure before starting the chemo. Dr. T asked: "You are not serious, are you?" I looked at him and said, "Yes, I am serious, real serious, and can I fly?"

For this act of boldness, I got a positive answer!

I booked the flight out on 16th November 2008, asking for assistance – to collect my luggage bag – from the airline and to have a seat nearest to the airplane toilet. Since I would be there for only a week, I knew I would need to spend this one week carefully and fruitfully. I sent out emails to ask for prayer and to book for appointments for a "prayer healing ministry", and counselling. I still needed some time to process the shock, the denial, and lost dreams. I strongly desired to come to a place of acceptance. Although I knew God was in control, and that He had carried me so far, I did have moments of down times and cried my heart out. Even in the recovery room, although I heard His voice and had a vision. I could not deny that I was disappointed at having to go through the process of chemotherapy. I prayed for the tumour to be benign but it turned out to be cancerous. I prayed that it would not spread, but it had already spread to my lungs. I prayed that I did not need to go for chemotherapy, but I needed to have the treatment. How could I not be disappointed or discouraged?

CHAPTER 2

The Source of Hope

At a time when my situation seemed hopeless, I was encouraged by this song, *"In Christ Alone"* by Keith Getty & Stuart Townend.

> *"In Christ alone my hope is found;*
> *He is my light, my strength, my song:*
> *...................*
> *My comforter, my all in all*
> *...................*
> *...................*
> *...................*
> *Till He returns or calls me home –*
> *Here in the pow'r of Christ I'll stand."*

In my low moments, I found comfort and encouragement from songs just like this one. I read the Bible and books *"Battlefield of the Mind"* by Joyce Meyer. Friends too, were great comforters. Since the beginning of this journey, I had spent lots of time writing journals which is my way of talking to God: –

On 16th November 2008 I wrote in my journal:

> *"When you pass through the waters, I will be with you,*
> *And through the rivers, they will not overwhelm you.*
> *When you walk through the fire, you will not be burned*
> *or scorched, Nor will the flame kindle upon you."*
>
> (Isaiah 43:2 NIV)

Chapter 3 of "*Battlefield of the Mind*" by Joyce Meyer says:

> *"It's easy to quit, it takes faith to go through......but just*
> *think, you have God on your team......make up your*
> *mind that you will not quit and give up until victory is*
> *complete and you have taken possession of your rightful*
> *inheritance."*

That encouraged me for the day and kept me hanging onto His promises.

Journey to Melbourne

In my 12th November 2008 newsletter, I wrote that "'time seemed to be at a standstill for me, my life had been turned upside down, no more long term plans, for only He knows my destiny, and I have to learn to cope day by day". I felt life had no meaning.

To give myself a motivation to recover, I was making every effort to see that I could travel back to Melbourne. On 16th November 2008, I left for Melbourne. My journey in the plane was good; I did not need to run for the toilet. That was a good start. As I had prearranged for prayer during my stay, I went on the 19th November. It was uplifting! I felt that I had hope again, looking forward to be a victorious person, walking out of this journey and sharing my testimony.

N and I had a night away at a House Cottage Retreat in Tonimbuk. The weather was wet, but we rested and enjoyed God's creation. Time flew by quite fast. Soon I was heading to the Melbourne airport on my way back to Singapore for a chemo journey scheduled on 27ᵗʰ November. It was hard to walk through the entrance of the departure gate at the airport. What would my future be? I didn't have a mother's assurance to give to my daughter. It was heart breaking to see tears in N's eyes.

The seven–hour flight was smooth, though I needed to use the toilet twice. However, the one week in Melbourne refreshed me and with all the friends and prayer warriors standing by me, I was ready for the next phase of the journey.

Tonimbuk Cottage Retreat

CHAPTER 3

Flight Ends, Chemo Begins

I landed at Singapore's Changi Airport Terminal 3 around 9:30 p.m. on Monday. The next day, B and I went to shop for groceries to stock up our pantry. The chemo would start on 27th November for three months, and then I would need to have a PET scan to see if the cancer cells were still active. From there, a decision would be made whether I needed a surgery to remove them or to go for more chemo.

B had quit her full time job and taken up a locum position in the hospital. This gave her the flexibility to take time off to go to the hospital with me and be at home, especially the first week of each cycle of chemo. That would also keep her from bringing back any virus from the hospital where she worked.

The 27th of November was a long day. B and I woke up early to prepare our meals for the day. Since it was the first day of chemo, we were not sure what time we would be back. So, we had a heavy breakfast, packed sandwiches for our lunch and concocted soup to cook in the magic cooker for our dinner. We left at 9:20 a.m. and arrived at the hospital around 10:30 a.m. While I had a blood test, B went to collect my PET scan report. We had to wait for the blood test report for half an hour before joining the queue to see the doctor. By then it was almost noon. They explained what they were going to do and what I had to avoid. Apparently, cold stuff like cold drinks and ice–cream were not to be consumed or to be touched. This was to prevent numbness, which is one of the side effects and medically it could precipitate peripheral neuropathy. Then I had to wait again for my turn to be called, to start the chemo (Oxaliplatin). By this time it was almost 3:00 p.m. When I finished, it was almost 5:00 p.m. I thanked God for Andrew's welcome ride home after a long day.

As I was having the chemo I felt "pins & needles" from my elbow to the wrist, where the medicine flowed through the intravenous (IV) drip. A heat pad seemed to help. But when I went back home, due to a lack of sensation, which is one of the side effects, I overheated it, and the affected part turned a reddish hue. It slowly subsided after two hours. Thank God! I prayed that I would not have nasty side effects, especially with the first intake of dinner after the whole day's ordeal.

The next couple of days were about adjustment – adjusting to food (yes again!), I should eat only fully cooked food. Goodbye sushi! Sayonara half-done steak!

B had taken time off until the 8th of December to become my care giver and personal chef. As I had to avoid cold stuff, it meant that I had to avoid the fridge too! No cold apple juice even on a hot weather. Everything had to be at room temperature or warm. I could not look for anything in the freezer or fridge in order to avoid the numbness. I learned to be creative. I tried putting on a jacket and oven mittens to get items from the fridge. I felt so clumsy wearing them. I thought of other creative ways with those thick oven mitts to get the things I wanted from the fridge. It was a case of "if there is a will, there is a way."

My life had been changed from being able to help others to being helped. I needed help for simple tasks like getting items out of the fridge and to defrost them to room temperature before I could handle them myself. I used to have energy to run around, but now I could not even spend an hour in the supermarket without looking for the toilet and resting on benches. On the brighter side, God had carried me through. He has never forsaken me even though I could not understand His purposes for allowing all these to happen.

Side Effect

I was thankful to God that I did not have many side effects besides having diarrhoea and a lower energy level. One Sunday, I slept the whole day and night. Because I still had diarrhoea even after the hospital discharge, it was not convenient for me to go anywhere. At the same time, due to low immune system, I had to avoid crowded places to prevent any infection.

Boredom

I was bored. My energy levels were low; it took me a longer time to read after the chemo treatment. I tried to be creative, I thought maybe I could do some sewing, but was not quite up to it. I tried typing prayer updates but it took me almost a week to do one. In the midst of boredom, I looked out of the windows in the study room and I discovered an eagle's nest on one of the trees. I did not know that was an eagle's nest, until I saw it soaring in the sky. Looking out of the windows to spot the eagle became my pastime. This eagle seemed to know when I needed that extra dose of encouragement. It would always be there at the right time as if God directed it.

Then, I remembered my prayer on 31st October 2008, where I asked God *"to hold me close and not to lose sight of me but let me rest on His Eagle's wings and ride high. Papa, I am tired, it hurts (physically and emotionally), give me the strength to journey this dark valley. Bring me up to the mountain, to have a breath of your breath. Dwell in me. Thanks Papa"*. I was amazed that about one month later, He showed me this eagle's nest and I saw the eagle soaring in the sky. Then, in my quiet time with God on 5th December 2008, I asked Him, *"Where are you carrying me to on your eagle's wings and what would I become – a writer, counsellor, speaker or what? Am I capable of doing all these?"* Later in that day, I saw a lovely rainbow in the sky.

On nights when I could not sleep, I would look for stars in the sky which are rare in Singapore's cloudy sky. Many days and nights turned into day dreams of the future and countdowns to the remaining days of chemo.

The Eagle's Nest.

The Eagle Soaring in the Sky.

A Perfect Rainbow.

On 8th December 2008, I went to the market to buy meat and vegetables. I did not have to look for toilet! I felt really good and it gave me the confidence to venture out again. I finished the last oral chemo tablets (5 tablets a day of Xeloda) on 11th December. After one week of rest, I started the second cycle on 23rd December 2008. That one-week rest was really good. The diarrhoea stopped and I was less tired. That break allowed me to do the grocery shopping and to take some walks during the early or the later part of the day. I was told to avoid sunlight during the chemo treatment period. I also started to sew some bags and posted them on my blog for sale. I sewed only when an order arrived. That helped to occupy some of my time.

I also spent lots of time reading books; one of my favourite is the very encouraging devotional book "*Streams in the Desert*" by L.B.

Cowman. Writing journals and updates to friends was therapeutic. I would download all my thoughts, emotions and feelings into the journals. I am glad I captured all these down into my journals and I could extract them to be compiled into this book.

"I know I cannot sustain this alone,
The pressure is just too much,
They just keep digging and opening the wound,
But I know that you are always with me,
You carry me on your back,
And soar in the sky!

I know this is my darkest journey,
With this unexpected sickness,
Grounded me in this place,
But I know that you are always with me,
You give me strength,
And make my day a Blessed day!

I know all these times,
All in the years,
How much you have provided,
And how you carried me through each crisis!

I know you are always with me,
Always carry me on your back,
And bring me soaring high in the sky!
Thank You my Abba Father, I love you always!"

(recorded on 21st December 2008)

The second cycle of chemo started on 23rd December 2008. My left hand was swollen due to the IV drips for the chemo medication. "pins & needles" occupied the whole of my left hand. I even struggled to unbutton my blouse when I needed to have a shower. I realized how bad it was.

In-between my second cycle was Christmas and New Year. Everyone was celebrating with lots of parties and food. I had a quiet Christmas and New Year. It was pointless to go to any of the parties for I could not eat most of the food and I would be looking for the toilet most of the time. So, I chose to stay home, did some reading, looking out of the windows and admired whatever was before my eyes.

God never failed to amuse me. On New Year's Eve, at midnight, I could see fireworks from Malaysia on one side of our study room windows which was facing west. On the other side, which was facing east, I could see fireworks from Singapore. In fact, I had the best view except it was a little far. Anyway, it did entertain me for a while and kept my spirits up.

Towards the end of the second cycle, I noticed that I had been running to toilet more than ten times each day. The tickling feeling from the numbness had gone down to my fingers and toes, and the sole of my feet. These were side effects from the chemo. The feeling of finishing the last tablet of Xeloda for the second cycle on 6th January 2009 was great, knowing that it was one more cycle down. It also meant that I could enjoy the one week rest before starting the third cycle on 13th January 2009.

The diarrhoea started to slow down once the oral tablets finished. I had learnt to adjust to doing things in between the toilet runs. For instance, in order for me to anticipate my next trip to the toilet, I would anticipate how long it would take me to travel from one destination to the next, using public transport. The timing was crucial as I would not be able to control my bowel movement. I started off with short trips of three bus-stops away from my home where I could walk into a small shopping mall, buy groceries, and then be home about an hour later. I also started to bake again and I did some household chores.

The third cycle was to start on the 13th of January and as usual the oral chemo drugs would continue for fourteen days. Then I would have a one-week break. After the third cycle I would then go for a scan, to see whether the cancer cells had been responding to the chemo and whether any other further treatment was needed. Up until that stage, I was still praying for a miracle to happen and that I did not need to go for any further treatment.

"You Raise Me" Up
by Josh Groban

> "......
> *You raise me up, so I can stand on mountains;*
> *You raise me up, to walk on stormy seas;*
> *I am strong, when I am on your shoulders;*
> *You raise me up... To more than I can be.*
> ...."

I first heard this song from the DVD that N gave me for Christmas; it moved me to tears and encouraged me a lot. I saw two sides to the lyrics of the songs: One was from N, the giver's heart. The other, was from the encouragement that I am strong only when I am relying on God, and He can raise me up to do more or be more than I could ever imagine.

Life had been challenging, and I struggled to keep myself sane and afloat. From my very busy and planned lifestyle, to a life of uncertainty and not knowing what to expect each day, this was very frustrating for me. I mentioned earlier that faith is the key factor in my journey. Deep down in my heart, I knew that He was in control and I learnt to trust Him more each day. Yet, at every moment of disappointment, I did ask Him, "Why me?"

Third Chemo Cycle

On the first day of the third cycle B and I woke up around seven in the morning, had our breakfast, prepared our lunch of a home recipe for Beef Bulgogi from a Korean friend, Jeon and waited for Sallie to drive us to the Singapore National Cancer Centre (NCC) around 7:45 in the morning. There were not many people at the queue when we arrived at the NCC. I had the blood test taken and waited for about half an hour for the report before proceeding to the consultation section. Again, I needed to take a queue number and waited for my turn. Thankfully, we were the first in the queue and saw the oncologist around 9:30 a.m. From there, we needed to wait yet again to be called into the surgical room where the doctor and nurses would insert the plug and then run the chemical treatment through the IV drip. The drip (Oxaliplatin) would normally take about two hours, and we would occupy our time with DVD movies (we brought a portable DVD player) and had our lunch there. That was our routine since the first chemo treatment.

The third and fourth days of the third chemo cycle were my bad days, as I experienced severe nausea. I informed Dr. T about the bout of bad diarrhoea that I experienced during the first and second chemo cycles. He reduced the Xeloda tablets to four a day instead of five. He also changed the medicine for the diarrhoea. Because I did not feel nauseous during the first two cycles, I did not ask for any extra nausea medicine. Lo and behold! An episode of bad nausea began on Thursday and worsened on Friday. B tried to buy the medicine from the nearby pharmacy. Unfortunately, a different type of medicine of lower potency did not help to stop that sickly feeling. On Saturday, she had to take a one-hour ride to the National Cancer Centre to buy the medication. Finally, my nausea was in control, and I was able to even type a prayer update. Without the medication, I was dashing for the toilet with diarrhoea and trying to vomit (imagine discharging through both ends!). After these toilet episodes, I would lie flat on the bed with little or no energy to pull myself up to do anything.

Since I had been running to the toilet and sitting on the throne so often, one day the thought of what happened to my "deposits" came to my mind, "After I pass motion, I flush it away, and where does it end up? Then, all things are processed in one way or another. Where do all these processed stuff go to? Does it become fertiliser or does it become soil? Does it end up in any animal farms or veggie farms or even household gardens? Who are the consumers? Have all the chemo drugs or other drugs taken by me and others been treated and removed in the process? How about those bad cells that were not destroyed? Will all these travel back in the food chain and back to us again?" I guess by now you all will have more questions than me… Have fun imagining. Let me know if you have genius answers! I knew it sounded disgusting but my life had been a roller coaster and I just needed to spice up my day. How else was I going to make the best out of the worst situation?

Of course I did have bad days, where I would do nothing besides running to the toilet, lying in bed or sitting in the study room to look for the eagle. Most of the time, the eagle would be there at the right moment, to lift my spirit up. The sight of it soaring in the sky encouraged me. I just could not understand the unstable nest. There were no storage places for their food, and yet, the eagle was soaring happily and freely in the sky. Why could birds feel so free and humans so burdened?

Friday 16th January 2009, was one of my bad day, which I recorded in my journal:

> "I felt very down, discouraged and felt that I am not getting any better. I tried to spend time in prayer and reading the Bible in between toilet runs and felt that I was just trying very hard to climb up this steep and slippery slope to the mountain top. However, due to its slippery slope, with not much energy, I managed to move upward three steps but slipped back two steps. At that point, I felt like giving up, and thought "is it worth it?" But, then I remembered all of my dear friends waiting for me at the mountain top, like my cheer team, and there I could hear all of them cheering and telling me that I could make it. How could I give up and disappoint all my friends who faithfully stood by me, prayed for me and cheered me on. Am I right? I decided, regardless how

tough that slippery slope, even bruises, scratches, whatever it took, I would get to the mountain top, out of this valley and do my unfinished work, unfinished course and serve Him according to His plan. Thanks friends, for being there for me."

God sent Rodney to visit me that afternoon. Rodney asked me what gave me the motivation. "Unfinished work, unfinished course, to serve Him and going back to Melbourne", I answered without much thought. I believed it was His timing for Rodney to visit and ask me that question.

The next day, still feeling tired and down with all the nausea and diarrhoea; I saw the eagle soaring with a companion. It was beautiful to see them soaring and I penned down this thought:

> *Soaring freely with no worries,*
> *Soaring with the flow of the wind,*
> *Enjoying the freedom and space,*
> *Life is so amazing!*

The second week of the third cycle was slightly better. The nausea was under control and the diarrhoea was less severe. I started to sew some coin purses, but felt tired after that and had to rest. There were times when I could not sleep in the night and I would spend my time in the study room (My favourite room!) to look for stars. I would end up writing journals, talking to God and, at times, I stayed up until early in the morning. When that happened I picked up books to read. One morning, I was reading the "*365 Day Brighteners — In your Time of Need*" devotional book by Dayspring, where this passage really spoke to me:

> *"May you have grace to press on...wisdom to guide your steps...and faith to see beyond the circumstances to the One who is cultivating beauty in your life."*
>
> (22nd January)

That helped me to see beyond and then I wrote:

FAITH ⟹ HOPE ⟹ MOTIVATION & DETERMINATION

I felt that with Faith I have Hope and Hope gives me the Motivation and Determination to get better. I hang on to my Faith regardless of the situation. During the tough times I poured my heart out — anger, disappointment, sadness and all to Him, knowing that He understood and would definitely carry me through the rough journey.

As mentioned earlier, after the third chemo cycle, I needed to go for a scan to see whether the cancer cells were responding to the chemo. The scan was scheduled on the 28th of January 2009, and I would know the result only about a week later. On the day of the review with the oncologist, I would be starting the fourth chemo cycle. At that time, the oncologist still thought that I would need another surgery. I was hopeful that I didn't need to. On 6th February 2009, I saw the surgeon who operated on my colon followed by the regular follow-up review after surgery.

Scan Result

The scan result revealed that the biggest cancer cell in the right centre lobe of my lung had shrunk from 0.7mm to about 0.3mm. The cancer cell in the lower centre lobe also shrank to close to 0.3mm. As for the other two, separately located on the right and left lobes, both had disappeared. Praise God for His Healing! I claimed His victory even though the other two shrunk cancer cells were still there. I still believed and trusted in Him.

Medically, the cancer cells could stay dormant or they could begin to reappear on the same spot and grow much bigger, or they would appear with a bang in much more numbers. To be safe, I was advised to go through the complete cycle, and wait until the cancerous cells grew again to a size big enough to be removed. At that point, I still hoped that after the sixth chemo, God would heal me completely and I wouldn't need to go for any more treatment.

Thankful

I am very thankful that throughout this journey, friends stood by me, prayed with me, lent me their shoulders to cry on, were my personal drivers and all the many things that each and everyone had blessed me with. Friends from overseas took time off to visit me in Singapore, too. All the acts of kindness that each did, made me feel very special and much loved. These were all my blessings from Him. I am thankful that He gave me all of you to be my friends. Thanks, friends! I pray that my readers, especially those who are walking the same journey as me, will have good support and will also feel being loved and pampered by people around you.

I am also thankful that B had been working as a locum, taking days off on the first week of my chemo. That really helped, as during the first week, I normally had bad toilet runs and nausea during the 3rd chemo cycle. Due to the side effects, I had to avoid all the cold things, and hence, was unable to get food out from the fridge to cook. Before going to work in the morning, B would defrost things that I needed to prepare for our meals for the day. This enabled me to handle the food at room temperature and helped to prevent the numbness in my limbs. I am equally thankful for N who took some time off from work to be here in Singapore. Now that she is back in Melbourne, she has learnt to be more independent. Thanks to all who have been keeping in touch with her, encouraging her and being there for her.

CHAPTER 4

Chinese New Year (CNY) in Singapore

Two days before CNY 24th January 2009, B and I went over to my brother's house for the traditional reunion dinner. CNY was quiet for me. I did not go visiting nor receive many visitors. I guess spending those years in Melbourne, where CNY is a regular working day except that one year it fell on Australia's National Day, a public holiday, I had become used to it.

In this journey, I could count the blessings of seeing long lost friends whom I managed to reconnect. Some friends had emigrated; hence, we were not able to meet up for a long while. Just before the start of my fourth cycle of chemo, we had a good catch up time for our girls' group; one of whom, I had not seen for over twenty years.

Every precious moment that I could spend with loved ones, was part of all the blessings I received.

The Fourth Cycle Journey

The fourth cycle of the chemo journey began on 3rd February 2009. God is always good! The first week was a real blessing as I did not have those toilet runs. I was thankful and I gave Him all the praise! I did make the best use of my good days, like doing housekeeping, sewing bags and even window shopping. I read my favourite devotional book *"Streams in the Desert"*. On 7ᵗʰ February, I was very encouraged by what George Mueller wrote:

> *"........our business is to HOPE in God, and it will be found that it is not in vain. In the Lord's own time help will come. ....our business is to SPREAD OUR CASES before the Lord, in childlike simplicity to pour all our heart before God...................*
> *For, I shall yet praise Him. More prayer, more exercise of faith, more patient waiting, and the result will be blessings, abundant blessing. Thus, I have found it many hundreds of times, and therefore, I continually say to myself, 'HOPE THOU IN GOD'."*

This reminded me of *Psalm* 71:5 (NIV)

> *"For you have been my HOPE, O Sovereign Lord, my confidence since my youth."*

Also remembering what I wrote in late January:

FAITH ⟹ HOPE ⟹ MOTIVATION & DETERMINATION

It motivated me and I felt that I could be a blessing to others even whilst going through this turbulent journey. Hence, I added my own spin onto what I had learnt:

FAITH ⟹ HOPE ⟹ MOTIVATION & DETERMINATION ⟹ DESTINY / AIM

I felt that when I managed to get to Motivation/Determination, I could set my goal and work toward reaching it. Further to this Faith, which I learnt to cling onto dearly, gave me this:

FAITH: **F**aith **A**lways **I**ncreases **T**he **H**ope!

I was thankful that I had many good days in this fourth cycle that enable me to buy materials to sew bags and the coin purses, shop for groceries, meet up with friends and most of all, to travel by public transport to church. I learnt to cope with the pins and needles in my limbs and to refine the skill of using the oven mitts to take things out from the fridge. With my left hand sore from the IV drip, I was able to do some cooking with my preferred right hand. I was grateful and thankful that I could cope and make the best out of the worst situation, owing to the fact that all my friends were with me. Local and overseas friends, even with time constraints, would come over to visit me. These are true friends who had been praying for me and who had given me all the encouragement that I needed .Thank you, Friends!

From "*365 Day Brighteners — In your Time of Need*" on 15th February, F. W. Robertson wrote:

> *"There is a past which is gone forever,*
> *but there is a future which is still our own."*

I found the quote by Robertson to be very encouraging:

> *"...past which is gone forever......*
> *a future which is still our own."*

A future, or an aim or even a goal brings us back to the equation that Faith brings Hope, Hope leads to Motivation and, finally, to realise the destiny, aim or goal.

In the Bible, James wrote in Chapter 2 verse 17:

> *"In the same way, faith by itself,*
> *if it is not accompanied by action, is dead."* (NIV)

Neil Anderson wrote in "*Victory over the Darkness,*"

> *"Faith is active not passive. Faith takes a stand. Faith*
> *makes a move. Faith speaks up."*

The Fifth Cycle Journey

The journey continued on 24th February 2009. During that journey, I had slipped downward to the valley, emotionally. Through friends upholding me in prayer, their constant calls, even overseas calls, emails, cards and those precious moments of meet ups, I was encouraged. They helped me to climb back up the slippery slope out of the valley. It was the loves that each of them gave that made me feel so loved and worthy and spurred me on to give my best effort in this journey to recovery. I could not thank God enough for having brought each of my friends into my life.

In this stretch of the cancer journey, it was as if I was hit by a tsunami. I felt that I was being slapped with hopelessness and despair walking out of the consultation rooms with bad news. During the review before the start of the IV chemo, I was told that I may have to do the seventh and eighth cycle of chemo, and that I also may need another surgery. The last scan report showed improvement and with that, I was hoping that it would continue to improve, and that I would not need to go for further chemo or surgery. I felt being robbed of hope. Medically, it would be better to have the surgery. I was frustrated, drained and I just wanted to be left alone.

I took time out on my own, just to feel His presence, to cry to Him, to ask the "why" questions and how long more towards the end of the tunnel. I even told God that I felt it was just too hard for me. I was on the verge of giving up. The next couple of days, I spent lots of time in this "cozy" place with God until I found peace from within. Though the journey was still uncertain, I trusted that He would carry me through.

On 24th February 2009, Andrew came around 8:00 a.m. to drive B and myself to the National Cancer Centre. Upon arrival, I had a blood test, and waited for the result before heading to see the oncologist. After the review, I headed to the procedure room for the IV (Oxaliplatin). By the time it finished, it was about two in the afternoon and Andrew drove us back home again. I went to sleep and only woke up much later for dinner.

I slipped further down the slippery slope. I felt really down, discouraged, and I asked God lots of questions. I told Him that I felt physically tired, especially after the toilet runs, and I could not sleep, even in the night. I would wake up at 2:30 a.m. or at other odd times unable to return to sleep. It was difficult to sleep because of the numbness in my arms and I could not find a comfortable position to lie on. My legs ached, too. The toes were numb with pins and needles. But God faithfully sent me encouraging emails and even calls from Melbourne. He knew when I was slipping backward, appointed the best person to call me and He sent the right people to visit at the time when I most needed. Even reading from books was encouraging, like this one from *"365 Day Brighteners — In your Time of Need"* on 1st March:

> *"Begin today! No matter how feeble the light, let it shine as best it may. The world may need just that quality of light which you have."*
>
> (Henry C. Blinn)

I wrote in my journal on the 1st March 2009:

> *"Papa God, I am struggling, struggling to keep afloat, struggling to find some certainties, struggling to see with my spiritual eyes, how to move on from here and what to expect. I cannot even be where I love to be. I cannot even enjoy what I love to do. What's life....meaningless?"*

I felt life was meaningless and crooked as I read from the *"Streams in the Desert"*:

> *"We may wait till He explains,*
> *Because we know that Jesus reigns.*
> *It puzzles me; but, Lord, You understandest,*
> *................*
> *................*
> *I cling the closer to Your guiding hand."*
>
> (By F.E.M.I)

I just agreed that there are things that I did not understand. Why my life had become so crooked? All I knew was that God had a master plan and He was allowing things to happen in my life, to mould my character to fit into His master plan.

From the book *"Never Give Up"* Joyce Meyer wrote:

> *"I don't care whether there seems to be a way or not. Jesus is the way; His Spirit lives in me; and I will find a way! .... Do not stop hoping, believing, and trying. Instead, say, I will never quit, I will never give up; I will never say, 'No Way!' "*

Due to the chemo side effects, I felt the burning sensation in my palms, fingertips and toes. I felt like I was on fire that it totally disrupted my sleep that night. The following day, was one of those "worst-of-all" days. I started having only about two or three hours of sleep, and I had more than twenty toilet runs. I was thankful, that B was home. She baked some muffins and pasta for lunch. Thanks Moyna, for calling at the right time. God knew that I needed someone to download and you called.

It was five months into my cancer journey. It seemed like eternity and I was nowhere near the end of it! I was still struggling with extreme boredom and toilet runs. But I learnt to appreciate every part of my body, even the intestines. The function of the intestine is so important, yet all this I had taken for granted in the past.

Reflecting on things I appreciate, I treasure Jonathan & Kate, Peter & Pat for squeezing in a stopover in Singapore to visit me, in the midst of their tight schedules. I am grateful to Angeline and Hannah for making those calls to me. God knew when I needed the extra dose of "TLC" (tender and loving care), and when I needed to unload my downcast emotions. My heart was made glad by each act of love.

I learnt that "investing" in friends were important. I used the word "investing" as we need to spend time like one spending time to invest in share or business. For shares and business, one invests to gain profit, but investing in friendship, one gains support emotionally, physically and sometimes, financially. In building friendship, we learn to understand each other's character, to help one another, and to be able to support one another in times of crisis. My heartfelt thanks to all friends!!

The Sixth Cycle Journey

Tuesday, 17th March 2009, was to be the start of the sixth cycle of chemo. I was praying that I would do better in this cycle. I believed that He has already healed me and I am waiting to see the manifestation of this healing. Miracles *do* happen in this century, even if doctors go by books and scientific reasoning.

On that day, B and I decided to take a train down to the NCC, rather than call our friends to fetch us. Our appointment was at 10:30 a.m., which meant that I had to be there by 9:30 a.m. for the blood test. That time would allow us to leave home at about 8:30 a.m., when the office peak hour rush would be over, and I would not be caught in a crowded train. We had been blessed with friends who would bring us there, waited for us and sent us home every time we went to NCC. Since it normally took two hours for the IV, and the waiting time could, sometimes, feel like eternity, for a change, we thought we could take the train and call a cab or a friend for our return trip.

We arrived at NCC at about 9:30 a.m., had the blood taken, and waited for about half an hour for the result before getting the queue number to see the oncologist. We waited for another two hours before our turn, after which, we went to the department where the IV was to be done. Again, we needed to queue. However, things were bad that day. Due to some unknown reasons, it was very crowded and the queue numbers did not seem to move! We were told to go for lunch and have a walk before returning. What place is there to walk at the NCC which is located at the Singapore General Hospital? Anyway, we went to have our lunch, found a place to sit down and watched

DVDs. But it was too warm to stay outside. At almost 3:00 p.m., we decided to go back and asked the receptionist, how much longer it would take. I was really tired. I had gone to the toilet a couple of times. The waiting area was crowded, and the seats were not at all comfortable to lie down or to sit for long. It was only after 4:00 p.m. that I heard my name called. I was told that they had a bed for me which was not the normal reclining chair. I was thankful to God. At least, I could lie down and take a nap during those two hours. By the time they did the preparation and started the IV, it was almost five. It finished around 7:00 p.m. We took a cab back and were thankful to God that we had not arranged for anyone to drive us there or pick us up. It was a long day. We had spent almost ten hours at NCC.

Dr. T. said that he was happy to do the CT scan instead of a PET scan on 7th April 2009. This was helpful, as it saved a fair bit of money. He also scheduled for a review a week later. By then, the scan result would be available. Decisions as to whether I needed the seventh and eighth chemo or a surgery to remove any remains of the cancer cells in the lungs, hinged on the result of the CT scan. That did not make a difference to me, as I still trusted that God would heal me and it would bring Glory to His name.

On one of my bored days, I felt that I was sitting in the valley. So, I decided to search the meaning of my name. Most say that it stands for "true image", but I always said that **V** stands for Victory. Subsequently I found this:

Meaning of Veronica

"**Veronica** is a female given name, the Latin form of the Greek name Beronice, Φερονίκη,[1] which in turn is derived from Greek *pherein* (bring) and *nikê* (victory), meaning "she who brings victory".[2][3] In medieval etymology, Veronica was sometimes wrongly supposed to derive from Latin *vera* (true) and Greek *eikon* (image).[4]"

(http://en.wikipedia.org/wiki/Veronica)

It states: "she who brings victory". For me to bring "Victory" to others, I must first be victorious. That kept me occupied for days thinking of what I wanted out of my "numbered" days. Of course, I wanted victory rather than being stranded in the valley. I longed to reach the mountain top, to serve Him again and to give Glory to His name. I may slide down the valley \, yet I could make the slow climb up again / "V"! So, I started trudging up the steep and slippery slope again with friends cheering me on toward VICTORY!

CHAPTER 5

Decision Time!!

THE day came. B and I took the feeder bus to the interchange to get onto the train to *Outram Station* where we could walk up the slope to the NCC or wait for the free shuttle bus to bring us there. Upon arrival, we decided to have a good exercise walk. We reached NCC around 9:40 a.m., took a queue number and waited with anticipation, for our turn. It was around 11:00 a.m. that we got to see Dr. T.

That was the moment that we all had prayed and waited for almost seven months. Although I was confident that I was healed, I did not feel comfortable being there. Doctors generally believe in medical and scientific healing not in miraculous healing.

The scan result showed that there were scar tissues from the chemo on the two larger cancer cells in the middle lobe of my right lung. It did not show any sign of the cancer cells. Subsequently we discussed whether the seventh and eighth rounds of chemo would further assist, and if there was any proven case of benefit from having the final two more rounds of chemo. "Was there a need to remove the scar tissue from the lung? Would the cancer cells be active again?" I asked. Dr. T called the surgeon for a second opinion. After another twenty minutes of waiting,

Dr. T finally said he and the surgeon were happy to see me again in two months' time. No seventh and eighth chemo or surgery! Hallelujah!

Just one week before the two-month appointment, I needed to go for a blood test and an x-ray, in time for my appointment. If the scar still remained as a scar, and the cancer cells were not active, (i.e. grown bigger or spread), I would only need to go for a routine check-up. Otherwise, surgery or further treatment may be required.

Thankful

I am thankful that God had brought me so far – for a time of rest, time to be with Him and trust Him even more. I thank God for His healing and His providence! I was thankful, too, that I did a fair bit of sewing coin purses and bags and I painted part of the house to get ready for the wedding of my daughter. I was thankful for *all* of my friends, who stood by me, prayed for me and encouraged me in this journey. I was thankful for the beautiful sunrise that entertained me on the mornings when I awoke early.

This is captured from the room where I spent most of my time when I woke up extremely early and spent my time until the sun shone fully......

That's the tree where the eagle lives. See if you can spot the nest!

Overseas Visitors

It's always good to have overseas visitors and have the time to catch up over a *cuppa*. Thanks to each of you Angeline, Sarah and Moyna for stopping by Singapore. The hugs, smiles, encouraging words meant a lot to me and had helped me build up the strength and courage to walk this journey. Your presence and prayers made lots of difference.

> *"There are times when encouragement means such a lot.*
> *And a word is enough to convey it."*
> (Quoted "365 Day Brighteners — In your Time of Need,"
> 28th March)

> *"I have been trying to make the best of grief and am just*
> *beginning to learn to allow it to make the best of me."*
> (Quoted "365 Day Brighteners — In your Time of Need,"
> 25th April)

Time for a Break

Since I did not need any further treatment except a follow up x-ray, blood test and review, I planned a trip back to Melbourne.

I arrived in Melbourne on Saturday morning. It was good to see N at the airport, to feel and breathe Melbourne's cool air. What a change in temperature–from the extreme heat of 37 degrees Celsius to the early winter and freezing "welcome". B arrived in Melbourne a week later for a one-week stay. We had dinner together to celebrate N's birthday. My two daughters and I had a one-week get-away. This threesome trip would be our last, as B would be married on 26th June 2009. I was able to spend twenty-six days in Melbourne, with my remaining time spent catching up with some friends.

Our Weekend Away at Inverloch

My daughters and I left for Inverloch for a weekend there. The weather was not good. It poured on Friday and Saturday, but the sun shone brightly on Sunday. Reluctantly we left Inverloch on that sunny Sunday back to Melbourne. We stayed in a unit that was a converted post office train. We managed to go round the town and to visit the state mine. Otherwise, we spent lots of time playing monopoly in the converted "post office" train. Both B and I always ended up in jail. Thankfully, it was only a game. The area shown in the photo was where the staff sorted out the mail.

I had a great time and was thankful that B could take time out to spend that one week with us in Melbourne. It was a special weekend away.

I was back in Singapore on 21st May 2009 adjusting back to the hot and humid Singapore climate.

I went for a routine check-up at Changi General Hospital which went well. I was scheduled for an x-ray and blood test on 9th June, and a follow-up review on 16th June 2009. The day of review came.

In Moilong Express (converted from old mail train)

The x-ray result showed no abnormality! Medically, I still needed to be monitored closely and was scheduled to have a PET scan on 18th August 2009. The review for the result would be a week later. This meant another week of anxious waiting.

I waited. There were times when I did not make it in time for the regular toilet run I had grown so accustomed to. What a mess! On 9th June 2009, I felt helpless and frustrated with my body system. I did not understand why I could not control it and I needed to clean up the mess! I asked myself "What sort of quality life is this?"

CHAPTER 6

Wedding Preparation

The wedding of B was confirmed for 26th June in Malaysia and 3rd July in Singapore. As the days drew closer, I needed to start preparing some traditional things according to the Chinese custom for weddings. I also started to prepare some local Asian finger food and froze them, so we could have them for the morning tea on the wedding day. Then the wedding party, relatives and friends who came early, could have some refreshment. N would be back in Singapore to help in some other preparations. That kept me preoccupied between toilet runs.

On 24th June, twelve of us from the extended family went to the airport at about 5:30 a.m. to catch the flight to Kuala Lumpur. The flight took about fifty-five minutes and we had to collect the luggage and proceed to the domestic terminal for transit to Kota Bahru. It took another fifty-five minutes to arrive at Kota Bahru. The aunties, uncles and cousins came in three cars to drive us to the hotel in Kelantan. By that time, I was feeling sick and a little nauseated. The car ride to the hotel seemed to me like forever.

At long last, we arrived at the hotel in Kelantan where the wedding would be held on 26th June. I felt very nauseated and was too tired to even go for a late lunch with everyone. So, I stayed in the hotel room and had a good rest. In the late evening, my tummy started to "misbehave" and drove me into those terrible toilet runs yet again. What a day!

There were things to prepare for the customary wedding. We managed to go to the shopping mall for some window shopping. The customary wedding on 26th June started at 9:00 a.m. This was followed by a wedding reception in the evening at our hotel's restaurant. We took the flight back to Singapore on 27th June.

It was an achievement! I thank God that I was able to travel to Kelantan soon after the completion of the chemotherapy. Although I still had the toilet runs and was feeling tired, I managed the trip well. Knowing that I would have a long travelling time, and that it was not convenient to find a toilet, I fasted from food and that really worked. I thank God that although I had the toilet runs on the customary wedding day and was feeling extremely tired; I still managed to stand through the tradition of thanking every guest there! I am grateful to God for being with us, for the journey mercy and for sustaining me physically and spiritually throughout the whole trip.

Preparation for Singapore Wedding Ceremony

Arriving back in Singapore, my body clamoured for rest from the several toilet runs. My tummy did not respond well to the food in Kelantan. But there were things to organise for the wedding in Singapore. All these tasks and toilet runs kept me busy.

The wedding day itself was a long day. I woke up early to prepare the traditional glutinous rice ball dessert for the bride and groom, and some snacks for visitors arriving early at our house. In our Asian culture, we had a "tea ceremony" (serving tea to the elders as a respect). Then, we proceeded for the church wedding, and had some finger food for lunch at the church. My needed rest came before the wedding banquet in the evening. It was a tiring day as I had been sneaking in-and-out for the all-important toilet runs. When they wanted to toss the bouquet, I was unfortunately, MIA i.e. "Missing in Action"! Thank God, yet again, for sustaining me through the whole day and night despite having close to twenty toilet runs!

Church wedding in Singapore on 3rd July 2009

Back to Melbourne

After the wedding, N flew back to Melbourne on 5th July 2009 after spending two weeks in Singapore for her sister's big day. I followed N to Melbourne a day after and stayed there till the 15th August 2009.

I treasured my time in Melbourne, enjoying my new found hobby: "Eat, sleep, play and spending time in toilet"! During that season in Melbourne, the weather was good for sleeping in during the morning. I always slept soundly until after nine each morning. I was refreshed with all the "Rs" – Reading, Resting, Relaxing, Rejoicing in His presence, Restoring my emotions, Reuniting with friends over coffee, Reorganising things in the house, Rewind during window shopping, and so on. Sounds good, doesn't it? Actually, time flew so fast, and it was soon time to return to Singapore.

In this journey, I realised how many friends I have spanning various countries. I felt blessed. Yet, shuttling between Melbourne and Singapore, always with a limited time frame in Melbourne, it was hard to contact or meet up with all of my friends.

Back in Singapore

I left for Singapore on the 15th August. I needed to have a PET scan on the 18th August, followed by a review with the oncologist on 25th August. I still had the "pins & needles" sensation in my fingertips and toes. I also had numbness and muscle tightness in my limbs. My right hand was the worst, especially my right thumb. Prayers had kept my spirits up. They kept me going.

I was too lazy to do anything even to go out since arriving back from Melbourne. With only two or three hours of sleep, sometimes I could not sleep well at night. So, I would go back to reading and checking emails. I continued this pattern until the 18th August which was a Tuesday. I had to wake up early to be at the National Cancer Centre before 8:50 a.m. Upon arrival, I went to the reception counter to get the queue number and waited to be given that "rose syrup" cocktail contrast dye. After that drink, I change into the special blue gown and waited for them to insert the "plug" on my hand for the scan. Finally, I had to lie down on a narrow platform that would move into that "tunnel-like" machine to scan my lungs and abdomen. Thankfully, there was no delay and all was finished before noon. Anxiety built up as days passed by until I could get my result the following week.

The dreaded or hopeful day finally arrived. This was verdict day. What can a patient hope when he/she walks into an oncologist's room? I really prayed that the medical report would be positive, i.e. no trace of cancer cells. That was not the case, I was told, "It is active and it is back". I was speechless and devastated. Shock set in. I could not believe what I heard. I wanted to know whether I would need further chemotherapy or surgery. Of course – it was not what I wanted to hear, but I needed to know. It turned out that although the cancer cells were back, they were too small for any procedure. I was scheduled to see the surgeon for a second opinion. Would the surgeon be comfortable to monitor me for another two months or would he want to remove the cancer cells promptly?

Many times, I walked into *that* room full of hope only to walk out covered with hopelessness, despair and discouragement. I wondered if God really heard the prayers. If so, why was I not out of the woods? I felt alone again "Are you truly with me, God?" I asked. I had slipped back into the pit. I desperately needed that life-line to be able to haul myself up again. I needed my prayers warriors who were my cheer team to continue to stand by me and cheer me on. During that pivotal moment – I really needed all of their support.

John 14:1 says, "*Do not let your heart be troubled, trust in God and trust also in me.*" This was one of the verses that I hung onto. There were times; I found it easier to recite it than to **do** it!

The next few days were spent waiting to see the surgeon on 3rd September 2009. I wanted to know what he would do. While waiting for this important appointment, I took "time out" to digest what I had heard, to recommit the whole situation into His hands, and to learn to trust His sovereign control. It was hard but with all the support I got, I trusted that I would be able to hang on despite any impending procedures and outcomes.

I disliked the word CANCER. It gave a label to patients like me. I was not sure how and when the cancer cells grow in my body but from now on, the armour of God would guard me. "Cancer" would now be the acronym for **C**hrist's **A**rmour **N**ailed **C**ancer, **E**mpower **R**estoration to the fullest in life. By the way, the word cancer is always the small "c". Christ is always the big "C". Christ is bigger than cancer!

I was reading the "*Streams in the Desert*" devotional book:

> "*Remember, our faith is always at its greatest point when we are in the middle of the trial, and confidence in the flesh will never endure testing. Fair-weather faith is not faith at all.*"
>
> (By Charles H. Spurgeon, 30th August)

This spoke to me, and made me question if my faith was just a "fair-weather faith".

CHAPTER 7

The "Second Opinion" Day

My appointment with the surgeon, Dr. A, was on 31st August 2009 at 9:55 a.m. B and S went with me. (*S, thank you, for taking time off to be there for me*). After the registration at the counter, I collected the queue number and waited for my turn. I finally had a detailed explanation of the scan report. There were five small spots on the lungs. Three options suggested: the first was to wait until November 2009 to see if there were any further growth or change in the cancerous spots; the second, was to do further chemotherapy; and thirdly, to go for surgery.

The doctor said that surgery at that point of time, was not quite justified. He could pluck out the cancer cells located in the right lung because they were bigger but he was not sure whether he could pluck out all those smaller ones in the left. If he was unable to pluck out the cancer cells during surgery, he might have to remove a lobe portion of my lung. Removing the lobe, would reduce the function of the lung. Waiting for the cells to grow bigger, and plucking them up like plucking a cherry, would be better. The immediate surgery option was out. I was only too happy to hear that!

The thought of having another round of chemotherapy was absolutely too hard to bear. And there was no guarantee that it would kill all the cancer cells, anyway. This option was out, too. He and the oncologist decided to happily leave me alone until 10th November 2009, when I would have another scan and review by both of them.

TCM (Traditional Chinese Medicine)

After much consideration, I decided to try "TCM".

After spending the morning at National Cancer Centre, B and I went to the TCM that was located at Changi General Hospital. As I was a walk-in patient, we waited for a long time. It was very interesting to hear the physician present the disease to us, and to compare the difference in treatment from Western Medicine. We were blown away when he asked me questions like, "Are you having some tooth pain? When you do your "big business", do you feel this and that?" Both of us did not mention any of these to him. All he did was to feel my pulse and peer at my tongue. It was amazing how he picked up those symptoms in a non-invasive manner! He explained that he would not be able to kill all the cancer cells, but he would boost up my immune system so that my immune system could do the "job". Sounded good, but I still trusted the big Him!

Thanks

Thank you my prayer warriors cum "cheer team" for always being there for me. This news was discouraging not just for me but for you, too. However, I still believed God would heal me, although I did not know how or when. I just knew He would in His perfect timing. I wrote in one of my prayer updates to all my prayer warriors:

> *"Actually, I also wonder: is it that my "cheer team" was a little too relaxed after receiving news from the last scan result? 'Aiyo, too relaxed la....' that's why 'satan' attacked again (in the form of the spots on lungs). Haha...*
> *(Too bored, so finding someone that I can blame)"*

Oh yes! I was bored and adding humour into my update, helped. I was surprised to hear that some of them admitted that they had been relaxed. I was thankful for their honesty. "Thank You, Lord for their love, concern, listening ear, encouraging calls, emails and cards. Thank You for the invisible but empowering prayers of those who trusted You along with me. I could not be where I am without my prayer warriors."

An Eye Opener

I had a review with the surgeon Dr. W at CGH in the morning of 4th September 2009. It was just a routine check and it was done by early afternoon. One of my nephews drove me and B to CGH. After CGH, we had lunch and we proceeded to the Singapore Arts Centre to see the "Dead Sea Scrolls" exhibition. To see the discovered evidence relating to the Scriptures was very significant to me. By simply reading the Bible and trying to visualise how those Scrolls, oil lamps and the coins looked during the time they were used in history, was pretty hard. Having the opportunity to be able to view some of those items before my very eyes was remarkable.

CHAPTER 8

Travel Bug Begins...

Since I did not need to do anything medically until November, I decided to fly to Melbourne. I departed Singapore on 12th September 2009. I had caught a travel *bug* to shuttle between Melbourne and Singapore like a migratory bird.

I stepped into Melbourne on Sunday morning, at about 7:30 a.m. I was rather happy that we were ahead of time, especially after clearing the passport counter. We were the first plane that landed in that hour. That meant, the queue for immigration declaration would not be too long, since I had to declare the traditional Chinese medicine that I was carrying. However, the container with luggage got stuck in the plane, so there was a delay of more than half an hour at the collection belt. By that time, the queue at the declaration was very long. Thankfully, when my turn came and after presenting the letter from my physician the custom officer simply looked through my items and cleared me for entry. N was waiting for me, and we headed straight home. I unpacked most of my luggage, had a quick shower and left with her for the 11:00 a.m. church service. After church, we went for lunch and I came back home to catch up on my "lost" sleep!

During one of my times out with Him, I read *Isaiah* 12:2,

> *"I will trust and not be afraid, for the Lord is my strength and my song."*

What an encouraging verse, even when I felt that life was still so uncertain. Below is one of the references that truly resonated with me. It was extracted from *"Streams in the Desert"* devotional book:

> *"Speak, Lord, in the stillness,*
> *While I wait on Thee;*
> *............*
> *............*
> *............*
> *Be not silent, Lord;*
> *My soul on You does wait*
> *For Your life-giving word!"*
>
> ("Streams in the Desert," 18th December)

A Year's Journey

In this one year, I read lots of books relating to people who had been through what I was going through, but not much was recorded of their emotions. I wondered if it was alright to feel disappointed, discouraged, despaired or just wanting to be alone. How would people around me, especially my loved ones, understand my downcast emotions which I struggled with? Below was an extract from one of my prayer updates that I sent to my "cheer team" and prayer warriors.

> *"Time flies fast, on the 9th October 2009, will be one year from the discovery of my colorectal cancer. It was almost one year, a long journey to me, it seems like many years. It has changed me in lots of ways, in looking at life in a different perspective. I have learnt to just eat, sleep and play. To make it sound better, to relax. I learnt to treasure each day, which I call 'my bonus day'. I discovered who*

my true friends are, friends I can count on for prayers, support emotionally, listening ears, a shoulder to cry on, or practical helps like transportation and many others.

It has been a tough and tiring journey, and I know I am not out of the woods yet. But I am very thankful that I have a God, who is my Rock and whom I can trust regardless of what happens. I remain thankful that He has given me so many true friends, and thankful for where I am today. I am thankful that I could go to Him and pour out my heart without being judged. Thankful I could be honest to Him with my true feelings and release all to Him.

During this whole journey, people frequently asked me some of the questions which I find hard to comprehend or answer:

FAQ (Frequently Ask Questions)

*Q : **"How are you?"***
A : "??" or Fine!

*Q : **"How are you coping?"***
A : "??" or Coping well.

*Q : **"Have you moved on?"***
A : "??" or yes definitely, I have moved on.

I found it hard to give a true answer, answers from my heart. Do people ask and just want to hear fine, coping well, moved on, or do they want to hear my journey of ups and downs? There were days when it was really not fine, when I struggled to face reality, hence how could I say fine, coping well and moved on? When I honestly told people how I felt (which was negative), I was thrown with Scripture verses, lots of theories and so forth. Yes, I could tell all of them. I did not need extra "dosages" of advice when I was down in the "pit". I was just being honest by telling my true feelings; all I needed was a listening ear, people who could empathise with me.

I know each of you love me, were concerned about me and those questions were asked out of love, I too asked those questions. Should I then give answers that soothe the ears, or should I be honest? Let me give you a scenario:

Imagine you were driving on a weekend away. You then come to this winding track road, and it happened to rain. That makes the track road muddy, a little flooded and you cannot see where the humps or bumps are. At this point you are driving slowly, careful about the humps and the bumps, trying to avoid any big holes, but it is hard to see because it is slightly flooded with muddy water. Then I call you on your mobile, asking you those FAQs. Will you tell me you are fine, coping well on that drive or moving on? You probably would not want to answer the call as you would not be able to concentrate at that point, unsure of what lies around the bend, or whether you would get stuck in the hole or in the mud. Am I right?

I felt that I was living in lots of uncertainties, one day I was fine, the next I may not be. Unsure whether I had moved on, for one moment the results seemed promising and the next I was back to square one. How could I say that I had "moved on", when I was still stuck with cancer, still not back to work, or even to my normal lifestyle.

Friends, in your lens, you may look at things differently, but we all wear different lenses; hence I do appreciate when you all next ask those FAQ, do respect my answers (for it may be one of my down days)."

Dear reader, I had been very open and honest with my emotions. I hope that for those who are going through the same journey, you will understand that having downs moments is part of the process. But do not stay down for too long. For those who have friends or loved ones going through this, be sensitive to patients' emotions, and give them the space to grieve, to be disappointed and to be discouraged. Be there to empathise with them and give them encouragement. Rebuking them or throwing at them heaps of Bible Scriptures or telling them what <u>should</u> be done, or what <u>not to do,</u> will sound like clanging cymbals. At least, they did to me!

Where am I with Hope?

The last eleven months had been a painfully tiring journey. Lost in the woods, with very little glimpse of light and unsure how long more this journey would last. I was hanging by the thread. Remembering how the Bible character, *Job* hung on to his faith even at his darkest moments, I was learning from him and the rest of the Old Testament prophets to trust and walk by faith in this journey. God gave me hope and all the prayers kept me afloat.

Philip Yancey wrote in *"The Bible Jesus Read"*:

> *"To believe in God means to see that life has a meaning.*
> *The meaning of that life therefore, according to Yancey.*
> *Is to not overly focus what's happening in that life itself*
> *but rather, on how it impacts others."*
>
> (Paraphrase)

As I was unsure about of my medical condition, I was not able to tell what my future plans would be. However, as Yancey said, to believe in God means to see that everything in *life has a meaning*; I began to look forward to what was in store for me.

A Time to Relax

In this journey, I learnt to relax and to catch up with sleep from sleepless nights. Even the scattered wild mushrooms amazed me. One reason I loved returning back to Melbourne was, I felt closer to nature, and I could just relax in the backyard, or at a café and have a nice cuppa.

We have different seasons in our lives. This was a time for rest, restoration and preparation before He entrusted something big for me to do in the next season of my life. The next season would be challenging. That was why I needed such a long rest.

Kinglake

During the Melbourne sojourn, I joined my church's "green teams" where we went to Kinglake, to clear the property and to replant the gardens of families that were affected by bushfires the year before. I felt blessed that God gave me the strength and kept my tummy well during that day, so I could help out. I thought that since my friends blessed and helped me in many ways, it would be good to give back to the community in need, whilst I was still able.

Time flew, and soon it was time to say goodbye to friends in Melbourne. I headed back to Singapore on 7th November 2010. On my return, I had a review with my TCM Chinese physician. Since I started the medication, my bowel movements improved and I did not have to run to the toilet that often.

Grateful Heart

I was grateful to all of my friends and family or "cheer team". Without their prayers and support, I would not be where I was, nor would I have had the opportunities to travel to and fro on my own. I am thankful from the bottom of my heart, especially to those who took time off to pray for me. I also appreciate friends who drove me around. I felt so blessed and so spoilt by all of them with all the yummy food they provided.

The one year journey changed my perspective in life. I learnt to cling onto God just like a baby. I also learnt to commit each of my *bonus days* back to Him and trust Him more throughout each bonus day.

> *"Difficulty is the very atmosphere of miracle – it is a miracle in its first stage. If it is to be a great miracle, the condition is not difficulty but impossibility. The clinging hand of His child makes a desperate situation a delight to Him."*
> (From "Streams in the Desert," 14th October)

This inspired me as I walked this journey clinging to Him. The thought of experiencing a miracle and bringing glory to His name in a simple situation does not make sense. It is only when we experience a miracle on *impossibility* that we would accept there is God in existence. Don't you agree with me?

PR Application

After a long consideration, I decided to apply for Australia Permanent Residency in June 2008. It was a long wait for the processing of my PR by the Australian Immigration. It took some time due to numerous applications. It was late October 2009, when I was in Melbourne, I received information that I needed to provide more paper work and submit to a medical check. I was not sure what to expect from the medical check. On one hand, I was excited about progressing in the visa application, but on the other hand, I knew it would be a big challenge due to my medical condition. In the meantime, I needed to submit an Assurance of Support.

When I returned to Singapore, I went to apply for the police check which would take about two weeks for a response. I went to have the medical check up done at the clinic accredited by the Australian Immigration Department on 20th November 2009. Considering my last medical review, I knew that I did not have a good chance of getting it approved. The deadline to submit all the required documents was by 7th December 2009.

CHAPTER 9

November 2009

An exciting and welcomed news awaited me on 5th November. I would be a grandma by June 2010. My heart leaped in thanksgiving to God for the extra time to meet my grandchild. What a blessing! I was reminded again about the acronyms "**FAITH**" (**F**aith **A**lways **I**ncreases **T**he **H**ope), and "**CANCER**" (**C**hrist **A**rmour **N**ailed **C**ancer, **E**mpower **R**estoration). God is Almighty and by putting on His armour, we are protected. He is also the God of the impossible.

Returning back to Singapore meant that it was time for my follow-up review. I went for the CT scan on Tuesday, 10th November and the colonoscopy on Friday. I disliked the one week waiting time after the scan before seeing the oncologist. That one week, always seemed like years. Like a pendulum, I oscillated from hope to despair and from faith to fear. 17th November finally came, and the result of the CT scan showed that the cancer cells in both the lungs had grown from 0.5mm to 0.7mm/0.8mm. There were two in the right lung and one (0.8mm) in the left.

Emotions

I was enveloped with disappointment. At the same time, I did not want to give up my hope and belief. I still trusted that He would heal me and that He still had great plans for me. I went back to download to Him. I told Him honestly how I felt, my disappointment, my frustration and that feeling of my world crumbling down once again. With the uncertainties, yet again, I was not sure what I could do. I told Him that I did not want to doubt, but I really would like to know if He heard my cries. Did He really collect all my tears? Did He hear my heart, and was He going to intervene? Had I not reached the maximum, or was He still stretching me?

I recalled the story on the death of Lazarus, where the sisters, Mary and Martha went to Jesus about Lazarus' critically ill health. Jesus said to them,

> *"This sickness will not end in death. No, it is for God's*
> *glory so that God's Son may be glorified through it."*
> (John 11:4 NIV)

When Jesus heard the news of Lazarus' health, He remained in the village where He was ministering for a few days longer. It was not because Jesus didn't care. By the time He arrived in the town where Mary & Martha waited, Lazarus was already dead. Jesus raised him from the dead so that all would know God's glorious and miraculous ways. Jesus is a God of power and miracles and He has sovereignty over death.

I was encouraged that in my journey, I could glorify His name in all my bonus days through my journals and prayer letters, to share my journey with people and encourage them. Thank You, Lord, that I could be your vessel. When I read *"Streams in the Desert,"* I was reminded again never to doubt God:

"Never doubt God! Never say that He has forsaken or forgotten. Never think that He is unsympathetic. He will quicken again. There is always a smooth piece of every skin, however tangled. The longest day at last rings out the evensong. The winter snow lies long, but it goes at last."

("Streams in the Desert," 19th November)

Surgery or Wait

The oncologist suggested that the surgeon would be the best person to decide whether or not I should go for surgery or to wait and monitor the tumour growth. I was given an appointment on Thursday morning to see the surgeon.

I disliked the waiting for results and the waiting to know what they were going to do next. I waited for two nights and a day, to find out whether or not I would end up on the surgeon's "cutting board". Finally, the surgeon said it was too early for me to be on "his cutting board". In his opinion, the cancer cells were not growing *that* fast. Waiting for six months to decide what to do would allow the small and hidden cancer cells, if any, to appear on the scan.

Of course, I was overjoyed, as some of you know that I was not mentally prepared for any surgery at that time. B and I left the hospital and went to window shop and had a good lunch. What a relief! I was really thankful to my Almighty God!

Thankful

I am grateful to all of my friends and others whom I didn't know who were praying for me all the time. Their faith and encouragement kept me going. They were there when I needed to unload and they allowed me to pour out my heart and be who I am. I love all of them.

I had two nights of tossing questions to the *"Hotline"* asking God ALL my "ifs", "buts" and "whys" through prayer. I wrestled with Him which helped me to draw closer to Him. It also helped me to feel He heard all my cries. By the way, this twenty-four hour "Hotline" is open to all. Thank God, for making this "Hotline" available.

I am thankful for all the extra bonus days, months and years. Thankful too, that I had the opportunity to see my eldest daughter get married and be a soon-to-be mother. I was blessed for the extra time that I could spend with N in Melbourne and enjoy her baking as her "guinea pig". I trusted that God would still grant me extra time to spend with my grandchildren and to serve Him again.

TCM and Trust

I mentioned earlier that I started taking Chinese Herbs to supplement my diet and to build up my immune system. I found out that it helped to control my bowel moments, and it reduced my toilet runs significantly. I was told that Chinese medication would take some time to "fine tune" the body's system, boosting up the immune system, which would then be able to control the cancer cells.

I struggled internally as to whether or not I should take TCM. By taking it, did I not trust God one hundred percent? On the one hand, I said that I still trusted Him, and believed He would heal me somehow and someday. On the other hand, was it wrong to think He might heal me through the use of Chinese medication?

Time for Reflection

As the end of the year drew nearer, and faced with uncertainties regarding my direction, I could only reflect what I had learnt the whole year, and to entrust my next season of life into His hands, He knew my future,

> *"…plans to prosper you and not to harm you, plans to give you hope and a future."*
>
> (Jeremiah 29:11 NIV)

I have learnt to lean on Him, to draw strength from Him each day, and whatever the circumstances, to be joyful and appreciative. Those eagles that He sent to entertain me had taught me many things through their simple lifestyles, their trust, and their carefree living. It was something that one could not comprehend – how much detail the Lord had taken into account when He created all the living things and the earth. The eagles always brightened my day, especially, when I was able to see four of them soaring together in the sky.

Just when I thought all was well and I could relax, reflect and respond to the next season in life, a nasty surprise sprung...

CHAPTER 10

Back to Hospital

I was admitted to the hospital on Monday night, 14ᵗʰ December 2009. I was writhing in stomach pain from the afternoon until late evening. I called B only when I felt I was getting worst. She came with her husband and decided to send me to the "A and E" in Changi General Hospital.

At the hospital, I had x-rays and scan. There was a blockage in my small intestine. I was given morphine for the pain, had drips and a nasal tube. The nasal tube was to extract all the "rubbish" that was building up in my stomach. That tube was taken out only on Wednesday. I was given "fleet" to remove all the waste from the bowel that was causing the blockage. Then, the toilet runs began once more.

On the positive side, this helped to keep my weight in control. Since they needed to "rest" my intestine, I was not allowed to have any food or drink for the first two days of my hospital stay. Then, they started me on clear liquid, i.e., water and really clear soup, on Thursday. I had soft diet with low residue for lunch and dinner only on Friday. Very boring food! The toilet runs stopped after lunch. From then on, I would be on a low residue diet until my tummy adjusted back. I was discharged on Saturday, on condition that should I have another blockage, I needed to be back to hospital again.

Still in the Woods

I knew I was not out of the woods. But I still trusted Him in every step I took and every day I faced. I was not sure about tomorrow, but I was certain I could trust Him to carry me through for He had been my HOPE. I identified with the Psalmist who wrote,

> *"For you have been my hope, O Sovereign Lord,*
> *my confidence since my youth."*
>
> (Psalm 71:5 NIV)

At that time, whether friends knew I was in hospital or not, it did not matter. I knew that each of my friends had been praying for me, it was their prayers that kept me going. I knew their prayers were answered, for I did feel His presence. I am thankful to all!

Sense of Humour

In one of my prayer letters to all my "cheer team" or prayer team, I wrote,

> *"I thought I should come up with this "rest package".*
> *Actually it can be called "slimming package or weight*
> *control package". What do you guys think?*
>
> *I know all of you are busy preparing for Christmas,*
> *whereas I have nothing better to do. So, by coming up*
> *with this, it might lighten you guys, at the same time to*
> *let all of you know that I am coping alright.*
>
> *Though this was all very sudden and surprising to me,*
> *I have learnt to trust Him in whatever situation that*
> *befalls me.*

5N/5D CGH Rest Package

1st *Night (Monday):*

Upon arrival at the reception (A & E), I will need to do the registration, and then will be greeted by professionals (doctors). After taking note of all the details for my reason joining this package, I was whisked off in a limousine (bed) to my well prepared suite (ward). In the suite, I was served with a cocktail (drugs/painkiller), and designer suit (hospital clothes). They also improved my image by giving me designer accessories (nasal tubes and drips). Then lights were off, and time to rest. They made every effort to see me through the night that I was well and comfortable (checking BP, temperature, drips, nasal tube and so forth).

1st *Day (Tuesday):*

Morning call was around 6:00 a.m. (when the light was switched on). By then I was awake, I had an early shower and if help was needed, housekeepers (nurses) were most willing to assist. The housekeeper also ensured that I had enough cocktail & accessories until given instruction that I had enough (by the doctor) throughout my stay. The professionals (doctors) came to check that I was comfortable and decided whether I needed any further services (like more x-ray or others). After that I was free for the morning. Oh, from 12:00 p.m. to 2:00 p.m. and 5:00 p.m. to 9:00 p.m., I was allowed to invite guests over for a chat. From 4:00 p.m., the professionals (doctors) would check on me again, to make sure that I was doing well (improving) and allowed me to have the luxury of a sip of 'H_2O'

2nd *Night (Tuesday):*

After the guests (visitors) left by 9:00 p.m., the lights were turned off to night light. The housekeepers (nurses) were busy again, checking to make sure I was comfortable and *ready for bed. Of course, they would make every effort to see me through the night that I was well and comfortable (checking BP, temperature, drips, nasal tube and so forth).*

2nd Day (Wednesday):

As usual, morning call was around 6:00 a.m. (when the light is switched on). Of course I was awake; I had an early shower, and then did some reading. The housekeeper (nurses) also made sure that I had enough cocktail & accessories. The professionals (doctors) had the routine check (rounds). After that I was free for the morning. From 4:00 p.m., the professionals (doctors) would call on me again to check that I was doing well (improving). They were happy with my progress, and decided to remove one of the accessories (the nasal tube) and I was upgraded from sip of 'H$_2$O' to drink wine (clear liquid) of 500ml.

3rd Night (Wednesday):

The lights were turned off to night light after 9:00 p.m. The housekeepers (nurses) were busy again, checking to make sure I was comfortable and ready for bed. Of course, they would make every effort to see me through the night that I was well and comfortable (checking BP, temperature, drips).

3rd Day (Thursday):

Around 6:00 a.m. the light was switched on. I had early shower (less queues), then did some reading and also played Sudoku (one of my favourite games). The housekeeper (nurse) made sure that I had enough cocktail & accessories. Breakfast (only Milo) was served around 7:30 a.m. and followed by the professionals (doctors) routine check (rounds). They decided to give me champagne ('fleet'), but unfortunately they gave me at the wrong end of my body. They also upgraded me from 500ml to 1000ml of wine (clear liquid) for the whole day/night. At 12:00 p.m. a bowl of white wine (I wish, it was crystal clear soup) was served (and allowed to drink half). I was busy visiting the 'throne' (toilet) after the 'champagne'. From 4:00 p.m., the professionals (doctors) would call on me again to check that I was enjoying my stay (any vomiting after the liquid). Then dinner (still clear soup) was served around 6:00 p.m. Soon after, the designer accessory on my hand started to give way (it bled), the housekeeper (nurse) was called, and it was removed. Thankfully, I was offered another one.

4th Night (Thursday):

The lights were turned off to night light after 9:00 p.m. The housekeepers (nurses) were busy again, checking to make sure I was comfortable and ready for bed. As usual they would make every effort to see me through the night that I was well and comfortable (checking BP, temperature).

4th Day (Friday):

By 7:00 a.m. I already had my shower, doing my reading or Sudoku. The housekeeper asked whether I still needed the cocktail (painkiller). Around 7:30 a.m. breakfast (still clear soup) was served and then the professionals (doctors) were on routine check (rounds). They were satisfied with my progress and decided to give me 'bonus' and upgraded me to 'LRD' (low residue diet). By 12:00 p.m. I was served with lunch (I did not eat that). However, I was encouraged to go and explore the 'hotel', hence I met B at 'Delifrance' for lunch (had baked potato). Wow, it tasted extra, extra yummy (actually I don't think it was nice, but for someone who had not eaten for 4 days....). The professionals (doctors) would call on me again in the evening to check that I was happy and enjoying my time (that my tummy was not bloated and no vomiting). Then dinner (minced meat porridge) was served around 6:00 p.m.

5th Night (Friday):

Night light was on at 9:00 p.m. Housekeepers (nurses) were busy again, checking to make sure I was comfortable and ready for bed. Of course, they would make every effort to see that I was comfortable (checking BP, temperature).

5th Day (Saturday):

By 7:00 a.m. I already had my shower, doing my reading or Sudoku and waiting for the professionals. By now the housekeeper knew I did not want the cocktail (painkiller), but for the service sake they still asked. Around 7:30 a.m. breakfast (porridge) was served and then the routine check (rounds). Being a good customer, they actually decided to offer me another day (until I have proper movement of bowel), but I told them I wanted to go home and should I need further 'pampering' (if my tummy bloated again), I would check-in to the hotel immediately. Hence I left 'hotel CGH' around 'one-ish', after I had lunch (porridge with fish and some tofu)."

Time Together

B did not report for work and had been spending time in the hospital with me. I appreciated that. Two of the afternoons, we were occupied playing Monopoly. On the weekend before my admission, we saw this travelling set at Toys 'R' Us, and she bought it. It came in so handy. He knows, right?

Before I was discharged from the hospital, I was sent to see a dietician, who told me that I would have to be on a low residue diet to avoid the blockage. At the same time, I also needed to be careful not to have too high fibre food; otherwise, I would be going to the toilet very often. I needed to balance the diet again. It was disappointing knowing I had very limited choice of food. I told myself I would work this out and trust God to bless the food I ate, turn it into nourishing elements to my body and, to not cause blockage or diarrhoea.

SPEM

"SPEM?" Well, Spiritually, Physically, Emotionally and Medically. I should say that I am medically no good, physically recovering, emotionally and spiritually still good. That is all because all of my "cheer team" had been praying for me and still do pray for me. Thanks!

Observation

I was in a six-bedded room and had one 86 year old lady next to me. I was thankful that my bed was right next to the window. The room was not air-conditioned but it was equipped with a fan above every bed. I was also thankful that He brought rain almost every night which made the room cool. Looking around the five other patients who were mostly above 65 years old, one or two seemed to feel lonely and would try to talk to anybody on any topic. The one next to me just closed her eyes and slept throughout, refusing to have food or drink. It saddens my heart to see so many ageing people in Singapore, living with family members but feeling so alone. I was told by one of the family members, that they all had their own families and could not find time for their mother. After surgery they would have to send their mother to a nursing home.

It makes me think, "What has happened to our Chinese tradition of looking after aged parents? Are we too caught up with the ""material" world to provide for the so-called "best" for the next generation that we have neglected the previous generation who has sacrificed much for us?" All these 70-80 year olds have gone through world war, lived a tough life to educate their many children and, now, they were being neglected. I saw the expression of this 86 year old, when the nurses tried all ways to coax her to eat; she just refused to open her mouth and simply closed her eyes to sleep. She was either on hunger strike or too depressed to eat. But when her children fed her, she would open her eyes, eat a little and would respond to them in a soft spoken voice when she did not want anymore morsel. I managed to see her smile to some of her visitors, too. I could not imagine her immense disappointment if she ends up in a nursing home.

Time with Nothing to Do

At night, after the storm and rain, I could look out and see lights of individual units of the Housing Development Board (HDB) buildings in Simei where my hospital was located. After two nights, I could roughly tell which families went to bed late and which families needed to wake up early (Hahaha..spying!). I could also see the flickering lights of the aeroplanes flying off and heading toward the airport.

The "nothing to do time" gave me plenty of opportunity to talk to Him. Sometimes, I could hear songs just playing through my mind over and over again, especially on nights when I could not sleep. In fact, it was a time to really learn to be still and listen to Him.

Disappointment

I thought I was doing well with my health and could be active again. In fact, I spent two mornings spread out during a week, to help an organisation to pack food for the needy. The people in this organisation started at 5:00 a.m. and cook meals for breakfast, lunch and dinner. The food would all be packed and ready for the van pick up around 10:00 a.m. for delivery to the various distribution centres. At the same time, I was trying to arrange for some counselling programs for the inmates – a busy undertaking for someone who still needed to rest. If that was not enough, I also offered to help in "a large ship with well-stocked library and crew ready to help meet needs of people in foreign countries"; when they were open to the public whilst docked in Singapore. With the new health challenges, it seemed unlikely that I could go there to help, or if I could even go there to say "good-bye" as it would be her last voyage. Sigh...

CHAPTER 11

Back Home from Hospital

On Saturday night, I managed to have a good sleep at home, with no disruptions, (as no one wakes you up to take your BP or temperature). On Sunday, feeling tired, I did not go to church. Thank God for this special time and "rest package" – the bed by the window where I could see the sky, the aeroplanes, sometimes even birds flying, and, of course the HDB flats. I could see the eagle soaring in the sky again and I trusted that one day, I would be like the eagle – soaring with Him.

Looking at the list of food I could and could not eat, added to my already boring life. I am the type of person who "eats to live" and yet I was greatly restricted. So, what choice did I have left? It was not the junk food that I had to forego, it was the so-called "healthy food" that I had to give up which was tough for me. Giving up greens like lots of leafy veggies, fruits like papaya, prunes, strawberry, kiwis and plenty more, even wholemeal bread (I was allowed only to eat only white bread) was a big challenge. *SIGH...*

Going Slow

I was going slowly with the "trial and error" experiment on myself. I started a log book, divided into four sections in order to record the number of times for "bladder clearance". The second section, I recorded the time for bowel moments. This included the degree like "a bit", "little" and "good amount", "hard", "loose" and "diarrhoea". The third section, I recorded all the liquid I took and, finally, the fourth section, I recorded the kind of food, snacks, biscuits or sweets. This system helped me to track down what I had eaten or drunk that would cause discomfort in my intestine and stomach. The log book also served as food reference should I be admitted to the hospital again. Recording them definitely filled my empty days.

Food and Drinks

It was hard to restrict myself from the fibre food. I had tried cooking different kinds of porridge: fish porridge, minced meat porridge, minced meat, fried bean curd, silver fish, and even chopped dried oyster porridge. I experimented with noodle soup using various ingredients, adding some greens which were not allowed. The half handful greens were chopped smaller and boiled until soft. Being Chinese, I missed eating rice. So, I tried rice a few times, meat dish and a small amount of veggie dish. There were much more things that I experimented with. Not all worked well for my system. The best that worked on me was fish porridge.

I tried some fruits juices and other drinks and found that some would give me discomfort. I had to forgo strong coffee and tea and was not sure how to make do without the good daily cuppa in Aussie Land...

Thoughts!

I woke up on 22nd December 2009 and felt that I had managed to walk the last fifteen months with lots of prayers and encouragement from loved ones, friends and books. I was reading from the devotional book, "Streams in the Desert," 20th December:

*". . . Eagles never fly in flocks; one, ...
God seeks eagle-men. No man ever comes into a realization
of the best things of God, who does not, upon the Godward
side of his life, learn to walk alone with God."*

With Christmas just a couple of days away, I felt alone and isolated. Was the isolation a time of "fine tuning" in my life? I chose to believe that God gave me this *time out,* so I could have time to "take stock" of my life. What had I done for Him in all these years that I was on earth? Was I ready to face Him, should I be called "home" now? In the passage, I read that God seeks "eagle-men". But what was the characteristic of an eagle?

The passage from *"Streams in the Desert,"* appeared real to me, for He had sent eagles right in my view and encouraged me in my journey. When I was given the chance to see two eagles soaring in the sky, I imagined one is me and the other is my Abba Father, and we had a great time soaring together.

The next day, I managed to board the ship, a floating library, to shop for books, CDs and say "good-bye" to her. The ship would retire from her mission due to stringent sea worthy laws rendering the 100 year old ship not sea worthy. Thank God that I was out of the hospital in time to visit the ship. I was grateful that the blockage was rectified without any further surgery.

Trusting in Him

I lost my freedom on the choice of my food. No, no! I should say I lost not only the freedom of liberal food consumption but I also lost my dreams, and I had to live with uncertainties. It did not seem to bother me much this time, as I still could enjoy the day-to-day simple life style and having time with Him.

I still believe He would bring me to the next phase of life, though I am not sure what and where. I believe in *Psalm 55:22:*

*"Cast your cares on the Lord and He will sustain you;
He will never let the righteous fall."*

I know He will sustain me and He will never let me fall, for He has carried me through the challenges of the last decade of my life.

Counting Blessings in 2009

I was grateful and I learnt to count blessings even in difficult times. One more year just slipped by. What could I be thankful in my journey of so many uncertainties?

Well, I thanked Him for the bonus 365 days where I saw B get married. God was there every step of the way. He gave me strength especially during the chemo treatments with no allergic reaction. He lent me His shoulder to cry on. He was my listening ears and He allowed me to download all my "junk" to Him. His providence even for my medical expenses was there despite the fact that I had stopped working since the beginning of my journey. The stamp of His Grace and His healing power could not be denied. There was much more to thank Him for... even though I was still in the tunnel.

CHAPTER 12

2010

With many uncertainties on the next turn and plan for a day, I was not sure what dreams or hope I had in 2010. I was encouraged by many friends to put my journey into a book. Hannah promised that she would be one of my editors. I began praying about it. On the first day of 2010, I asked God for confirmation about compiling my thoughts, feelings and my prayer letters into a book, so I could encourage readers who are going through the same journey as me.

When I felt alone, emotionally drained out, and discouraged by reports based on medical science, I learnt to look to a brighter side and to keep a positive attitude. Reading and pondering *"Streams in the Desert,"* during this winding journey, encouraged, refreshed, and kept me going each day. For instance, the entry of 5th January, *says "When nothing to lean remains, strongholds crumbled, nothing is sure, but God still reigns.... better walk by faith than sight".* This was a good reminder that no matter what happened to me, God would still reign and all I needed to do was to walk by faith. The rainbow I saw on 6th January 2010 was so lovely. Just like Noah, the rainbow was God's reassurance to me of His promises. Thank You, Lord for Your amazing love!

Make the Best of my Time

I decided to spend my good days cleaning up the walls, cupboard, windows and paint one of the rooms. This kept me occupied as I could only do a small portion at a time. I had a follow-up review after being discharged from the hospital for that blockage of the intestine. I had surprise visitors from Melbourne *and was thankful to Kate.*

The beauty of His creation always made me feel His greatness, His power, and the importance of each of us to Him.

"Stillness/Boredom

Being still, nothing to do;
Looking through the window's still,
Feeling the breeze, hearing the rain,
Waiting in vain.

Being still, nothing to do;
Hearing the birds sing,
Admiring the eagles soaring in the sky,
And then resting in its nest and be still.

Being still, nothing to do;
Hoping for a glimpse of rainbow,
The blinking of the stars,
Which bring hopes from afar.

Being still, nothing to do;
What's life without You,
You have been my all,
And my Hope and future lay in You!"

(wrote this on 22nd January 2010)

Scan and Review

On 2nd February 2010, was the review of the scan result that was done on 25th January 2010, it was the day to face reality. The prognosis was that the cancer cells were still growing but *slowly* (I was very thankful for that). The biggest one had grown from 0.75 to 1mm. I was scheduled to meet the surgeon on 8th February 2010 to discuss whether he thought it was time to remove them or to continue to wait. My planned trip to Melbourne would depend on it.

How I Kept Myself Busy

It all started with pineapple tarts to eat. Then B and I thought "Why not post it on Facebook and sells to friends?" Guess what? Orders came in and that kept me sufficiently busy.

N came back and we went to Krabi for three days and two nights. We had a great time and lots of fun. N left on the weekend and would apply for leave to be back in Singapore if I needed to go for the surgery. It felt great to have time out with N before the results and the final decision, "To cut or not to cut?" *That* was the question?

At Krabi

Final Verdict

8th February 2010 came, Dr. A suggested that I *should* go for surgery and he fixed the date to 17th March 2010. He described the procedure with a sense of humour and said it was like "Cherry Plucking". It also made it sound non-surgical to me. I would need to be at the hospital for pre-operation tests on 10th March 2010 and then, to be admitted on 16th March 2010 in preparation for the surgery the next day. My plan for a trip to Melbourne had to be postponed until I recovered from the surgery.

"Cherry Plucking"

I started counting down the days for the "farmer" (surgeon) to pluck the "cherries" (cancer cells). Not that I was excited about it, but I just want to get it over and done with. I guess you would like to know how I felt and how I cope with the news of this surgery. Well…

Do you know how cherry plucking goes in the hospital? Should I put it in a fun way for this surgery? Huh? Do some of you love to pluck cherries? Here is how it is done. As the "cherries" were bigger in the right side of my lungs, the surgeon would use the keyhole method to harvest those "cherries". Since the left side was a little problematic, he needed to go in and used his hands to feel (sounded disgusting). He would cut me from the side (not sure how), and he would work his way from there. My body became the farm and the surgeon the farmer who would harvest those "cherries". I was sure I did not want to buy or even eat those "cherries". Sounded *yucky*, right?

I would say I was mentally more prepared for this surgery than the previous one in October 2008 when they removed the tumours from the colon.

Of course, I felt disappointed. Why didn't the Almighty God just wave His magic wand and remove the cancer cells? Why did He allow me to go through *another surgery* to experience the pain that surely followed? But again, who am I to question my Almighty? I still believed that He had a reason to allow me to go through this journey. He would heal me in His time and bring Glory to His name!

101 Ways to Fill my Days

Time is fleeting. Once I awoke, there was not much done in a day, night fell, and, again, another 24 hours flew by. Below was an inspiration on a paint brush which I wrote in one of my prayer letters.

"I bought a small can of paint to paint one of the toilet walls. Somehow I noticed the paintbrush. I bought this paint brush around May of 2009 and painted the dining area of my home. When it was new, the strands of 'hair' from the brush kept sticking out. However, by that time it was just good to use although it appeared in a worse but salvageable condition. But with closer inspection, it looked very-worn out and didn't seem to be able to last much longer.

At that moment, I felt like I was the paint brush, painting His big picture. Being the paint brush, I have no glimpse of what the wall or picture will look like, but simply to do my part. At times, I do give my painter (Almighty God) some pain in the form of the need to remove that strand of 'hair' (my sins) that came out of the brush (my daily life and choices). Then I realised that the brush was comfortable and usable, it made my painting easy. It reminds me that when I am obedient, I will be usable by my Almighty God for His Kingdom. And of course the day will come, when the paint brush wears away and that is also the time when my time is up and it is time for the next generation to carry on."

Myself

As I felt encouraged by friends, pastors, and all my prayer partners, I also felt that people praying for me needed to be encouraged too. Hence my prayer update began:

"I know this journey has been a long journey not only for me but also for all of you praying for me. I am thankful that all of you are concerned regarding 'how I feel about the up-coming surgery', and the pre-op and the post-op arrangement. Thanks for all the thoughtfulness. I am really thankful that He has given me all of you in my life.

I also pray that all of you will not be discouraged as I do need to go for another surgery. It is not that He has not answered all the prayers. It is something that all of us will not understand at this point of time. I still believe He has answered all our prayers and He will heal me and bring Glory to His name, but in His time and not ours.

For the surgery to follow, I have peace and I am looking forward to be out of the hospital and worshipping with you all again. And for those far away, I am looking forward to see you all again. Thanks once again and I love all of you."

"Therefore I tell you, whatever you ask for in prayer, believe that you have received it, and it will be yours."
(Mark 11.24 NIV)

I started to think of the title for this book and to plan what I would like to share with my readers. Finally on 23rd February 2010, I started to draft the outline of this book.

My devotional book, wrote:

"Troubled on every side, yet not distressed, perplexed but not in despair, persecuted, but not forsaken, cast down but not destroyed. Be of good cheer."
(Taken from "Streams in the Desert," 28th February)

Although I had gone through this rough journey, I knew and I saw others who were going through a tougher journey than mine. I convinced myself to be positive, to believe that He heals, and not to feel cast down or troubled but to "be of good cheer". I decided to pen my journey into a book, with the hope that this book will encourage readers to *be strong, think positive* and to *enjoy each "bonus" day to its fullest in the midst of turmoil.*

On 10th March 2010, I underwent the pre-operation test: blood test, ECG, X-ray and lung-function test, one week before the surgery.

I wrote in my journal on 12th March,

> *"A star that seems so far,*
> *Yet always brings a smile,*
> *A star bright & sparkling,*
> *Always brightens my night,*
> *And sparks my hope.*
>
> *A star that seems so far,*
> *Yet touches my heart.*
> *That star seems far,*
> *Yet faithfully answers my call,*
> *Nightly, there Watches over me,*
> *Giving me the comfort & peace that I need.*
> *Thanks Almighty for sending that star!"*

This was just a thought to share with all of you. Actually, it was my pastime to look for that very same star since returning to Singapore. It was hard to leave those bright sparkling stars that were more clearly visible in Melbourne, but God kept me cheerful in Singapore by sending some to hover outside my windows, whether at home or in the hospital.

Two days before I was admitted to the hospital, I bought myself a laptop in an IT show. I planned to bring the laptop with me, so when

I was transferred to the normal ward, I could send emails and updates to friends and my "cheer team".

Mentally prepared for this surgery, I was admitted to the hospital late afternoon of 16th March 2010 after a good lunch. Although, I did not sleep well that night, I told myself that I needed a good rest. I was up by 6:00 a.m., did some light reading and recording in my journal before showering to change into the surgical gown.

CHAPTER 13

Second Surgery

I was thankful that both sides of my lungs were operated on through the keyhole surgery method. There was no need for an open surgery on one side of my lungs. The surgery was completed in about three and a half hours. The surgeon managed to harvest a total of six "cherries", four from the right side and two from the left lung.

I was in the theatre around 7:30 a.m. After the surgery, I rested in the recovery room until evening, where I was transferred to the High Dependency ward. Since I was given morphine for the pain, my body reacted badly. I was dizzy most of time, experienced nausea and complete loss of appetite. Even sips of water would cause me to vomit, which in turn, caused pain and discomfort to my lungs. On the morning of 19th March, they moved me back to the general ward.

Although I had the laptop, I was too drowsy and too tired to even sit up and talk until the third day when I managed to type an update to my "cheer team". I felt good this time. Of course, all surgery wounds are painful. This time around, despite the pain, it was more bearable compared to the colon surgery in October 2008. The main thing I learnt to cope with after this surgery was tiredness and breathlessness. Since the surgery involved both of the lungs, I was easily short of breath.

New challenges during recovery, made me appreciate *every* breath I took. I meant every breath! It involved enormous exertion to speak even a sentence the first few days after the surgery. It was also gigantic effort to walk even a short distance. Lifting up my arms was not only painful but extremely tiring. Everything required a great deal of effort. But I was thankful for my God who conquered all, who had been so faithful and who had carried me through. He kept me going. He lightened my load through His grace.

Discharged from Hospital

During the doctor's morning rounds on Sunday, 21st March 2010, I was told that I could be discharged in the afternoon. Praise God! It was only the fourth day after surgery. I was thankful that I could go back for I had a room-mate who would sleep talk (and loudly too!) and another who snored heavily.

Saturday night was not a good night for me, because I had irritable throat and it kept me awake coughing through the night. I was more than happy to leave the hospital on Sunday afternoon. N, who arrived on Saturday mid-night, came to the hospital. We left the hospital for home after collecting the medication from the pharmacy.

By the time we were back, it was past 1:00 p.m. and I was feeling tried. In the evening, N went for a friend's wedding dinner. I had a home cooked dinner by *Chef* B, followed by all the medication before having an early night's rest. As I had all the dressings removed, I could see all the bruises from the surgery and some skin irritation from the plaster they had used during the surgery. B helped to apply the medication on those places that I could not reach. I would miss my chef as she and her hubby would be leaving for a year's overseas job posting within the next couple of days.

How to Keep my FAITH Burning?

Time flew. Battling cancer slowed me down. It also give me time to reflect on my journey in a *fallen* world – what I have done, what other things I would love to do and have not done, and to question whether or not I was on the right *track* with God. To use an accounting analogy, it gave me time to "take stock" of my life. This manner of reflection, gave me plenty of encouragement and strength to cling to Him and to trust Him even more for my future despite the uncertainties. I still believed that my God was ever in control of my life.

My world had turned upside down since 9th October 2008, when I discovered the initial bleeding that led to a cancer diagnosis, surgery, chemo, and now another surgery. What is life to me? It is by Grace that I am still around; it is He that has carried me thus far.

Of course, there were times when I found myself in the depth of despair. But it was in this somewhat bottomless pit that I found God so real, faithful, and *always* there for me. I was stripped of all my security, my pride and dignity in order for me to truly discover the beauty of an intimate and trusting relationship with Him.

Stripped of All

What is the look of pride and dignity when you are sick in bed? Lying in bed with tubes all over my body, wearing undies was just impossible! What about my clothing? I felt so hopeless and helpless when a bedpan was required.

I stopped the TCM medication before the surgery. I was put on antibiotics soon after the surgery. My body system reacted with bad diarrhoea. "History" repeated itself with all the toilet runs, even during sleep. I could not walk as quickly as before and there were times when I would make a mess. Imagine the indignity of it all!

I was helpless, frustrated, and angry with myself for not being able to exercise control. Then, I felt that I should, at least be thankful that I was still able to clean up the mess and have a shower. Given that Singapore is so hot, it didn't matter how many times I showered. There were many who could not even clean themselves, let alone the mess they had made. *Am I right that I should still be thankful?*

After Surgery

Due to the toilet runs, I did not go out much. I kept wondering, "Could I make it to the next stop if I needed to use the toilet in the bus or the train?" So, I hardly dared to venture out of the house, except those obligatory trips to the doctors. Finally, on Monday, 29th March, I went back to the TCM medication and stopped taking the painkiller and antibiotics. On the second day after the TCM medication, the diarrhoea stopped. I felt so much more relaxed, relieved and it gave me the courage to walk to the local supermarket. Thank God the toilet run belonged to "history," once again.

Visit to Dentist

Just a few days after coming back from the hospital, one of my molar teeth chipped off. I am not sure if it was partly due to the surgery because they had to put a tube into my mouth. After asking my dentist to kindly squeeze me in for an appointment, he gave me a Saturday noon, the 27th March. But on Saturday morning, his nurse called and asked me to go as soon as I could. Because the clinic was in the city, and to cut cost on travelling, I took the public bus. However, not even half way through, I felt sick in the bus. I decided to alight from the bus and hailed a taxi. God is good! He sent a new, maxi type and comfortable taxi with a thoughtful driver. I thought, I must have looked really sick and pale because the driver told me to recline the seat if I needed to. He also gave me a fare discount. What a blessing! Another blessing awaited me at the dentist. He only took five minutes to fix my tooth and he did not charge me. In the MRT, on my way back, I mused, "Thank You God. You take care of all my needs."

Review on 5th April

The appointment for surgical review was on 5th April 2010. I arrived at the Singapore General Hospital at 8:10 a.m. I waited for about half an hour before the x-ray was done. Then I proceeded to the other level of the building for the review. Good news! Dr. A was happy with the healing of the wound. I was told that I didn't have to see him again unless there was any major issue. From there, I proceeded to another room to have the stitches removed. Now, at least the wound looked much better, unlike the first few days where I looked so brutally abused with lots of bruises and swelling. My next review was with the oncologist around June 2010.

What's Next?

With all the reports done, I booked my flight to Melbourne. During this period, I met up with a dear friend and discussed about the writing of this book, the theme, title and much more. We were excited about it!

Below is an extract from the book: "*Streams in the Desert,*" 8th April:

> *[George Matheson, the well-known blind preacher of Scotland, who recently went to be with the Lord, said: "My God, I have never thanked Thee for my thorn. I have thanked Thee a thousand times for my roses, but not once for my thorn. I have been looking forward to a world where I shall get compensation for my cross; but I have never thought of my cross as itself a present glory. Teach me the glory of my cross; teach me the value of my thorn. Show me that I have climbed to Thee by the path of pain. Show me that my tears have made my rainbow."]*

It is a beautifully written prayer. I realized that I, myself, have not thanked God for my thorn and, like George, to learn the value of my thorn.

Stress

Somehow in the month of May and June, I went through many roller coaster rides emotionally. With uncertainties in the future, I felt that my loved ones around me had been affected, too. They also needed the space and time to come to terms with my journey and to be able to accept the change in my next season of life.

Due to my medical condition, my application for Australian Permanent Residency was not to my favour. So, I withdrew my application. It was very disheartening! Although there were lots of disappointments, I still needed to learn to release all of them to God and trust that He would carry me through this turbulence.

In Singapore, we have karung guni men. They are people who pay a minimum token amount for the old newspapers, cardboards, broken down electrical appliances and many others. One day, as I was walking below my apartment, I noticed this karung guni man. He was shouting "Karung guni", pressing the hand horn and, at the same time, looking upward to see if anyone heard his call. If the flat owners would wave to him and would respond by shouting back from the units above, he could go up to get his goods. If he was not attentive, he may miss some of his potential customers. That inspired me! It reminded me that I should always keep my focus on looking up to God, and being attentive to His voice, especially in response to my distress.

Time in Melbourne

Each trip to Melbourne seemed to be a journey toward closure. I started to pack some of my things in boxes and gave some away. In the midst of doing that, I realised that I did not have as much energy as I used to. It could be due to the recent surgery or even due to age (although I do not believe that!). I only did a small bit but wished I was able to do more. Time just flew and I was due to be back in Singapore, for all the medical reviews again.

CHAPTER 14

Medical Review

On 11th June 2010, I had a routine follow-up review at Changi General Hospital where I had the colon surgery in October 2008. It was just to find out if there was any other issue after my last admission for the intestinal blockage, and also to schedule the next colonoscopy for the end of November.

The next medical examination would be on 22nd June 2010. I needed to do an x-ray before the review with the oncologist. I was thankful that the x-ray report was good. It showed only the scar from the surgery and nothing else. I was medically cleared subject to close monitoring. The following appointment would be in early October when I needed to have a CT scan.

> *"Faith is to believe what we do not see, and the reward of this faith is to see what we believe."*
> (Saint Augustine 24th July, from "Streams in the Desert")

Bundle of Joy

My first grandchild was born on 15th June 2010 in Taiwan. I flew off to Taiwan to meet my granddaughter on 27th June 2010 where I spent a few weeks. Since it was my first trip to Taiwan, I ventured out on my own to visit some of its attractions.

Introducing...

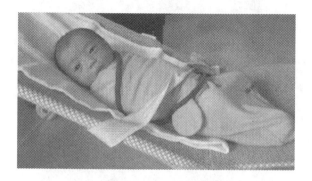

The bundle of joy...

Taiwan

In June the weather in Taiwan was hot and humid as it was summer then. I simply did *not* enjoy going out. Nonetheless, I spent one late afternoon and evening at Taipei central where I did lots of window shopping and enjoying the benefit of the shopping centre's air-conditioner. I explored Ximenping, Shilin and Wanhua commercial districts. Many night markets served a variety of local food and products. I tried the Taiwanese fried oyster for dinner and ice cream with peanuts, shaved into powder form, and wrapped with spring roll pastry. Oh yes, I went to this "Modern Toilet" restaurant for a meal. Would anyone dare to try it?

Thai Curry Set.

"Chilling Out"

I was back in Singapore for a month or so before I flew to Melbourne to enjoy the cooler weather. It was a time of catching up with friends and *"chilling out"* in the cool weather. It was good timing that I was back in Melbourne. On 28th October, I joined the church's "green team" again to help in the gardening and other clean up for the bush fire victims' families. It was good to see the families that we helped after the 2009 bush fire and to see how much the area had changed. The warmth and openness of the families affected by the bush fire, made me recognize that they had a part in the process of God's recovery for me.

During my first clean up visit, the gum trees were so badly burnt and they looked as good as dead. One year later, they had new branches and leaves were growing beautifully. They had passed the test of fire. Other then black burnt trunks of the tree, you could not tell that the tree had gone through a tremendously arduous recovery and growth journey. Do you sense the analogy?

God is great. He created things in great details. He created the trees growing in bushfire affected areas which are able to grow again after going through the searing ordeal of fire. God gave these trees the ability to bounce back to life even in the most horrendous of circumstance. Reflecting on my own life, I began to understand God had created me to endure the journey that I was on, and He had a purpose for allowing it to happen. I believed He had promised to carry me through and had great plans for me. In my journey, I *will* regrow just like those gum trees, and people will see the beauty of God through the process.

My youngest daughter took a two-week holiday to visit her new born niece in Taiwan, and I got the use of her car while she was away. The weather at that time had been cold and wet and I did not have the chance to really get to my favourite garden to pass my time. Sigh! There were nights when the wind was strong and her house experienced some disruption in power services. This left me feeling physically lonely but full of the assurance and peace of God's reality and presence.

Inner Healing

When I was doing a counselling degree in Melbourne, I learnt about the ministry of inner healing. The inner healing ministry aims to help people deal with their emotional pain, which may have been caused by negative experiences in life or difficult illnesses.

> *"The belief that there is value in inner healing ministry is based on Biblical truths. In Psalm 34:18 we read, "The Lord is close to the broken-hearted, and saves those who are crushed in spirit." It is clear from this and many other scriptures that we can be hurt by others and by circumstances in our lives. It is also clear that God loves us and cares for us in an active way. He listens to prayer and is able to answer. He is also able to intervene and heal. Isaiah 53:5 prophesies about Jesus and his redemptive work on the cross. It says, "... by his wounds we are healed." This statement refers to the damage that is done to us through the sin that we commit. This restoration includes healing from the negative effects of sin committed against us, or from the effects of damaging situations. If we accept that we can carry hurt from past (and present) experiences, and that God cares about this and is able to heal us, it makes sense to pray and invite the Spirit to come in healing and help those who are damaged."*
> (http://www.walking-wounded.net/html/inner_healing_prayer.html)

The process of inner healing began at the end of 2008. After the first surgery, but before going through the chemotherapy, I went back to Melbourne to hand over the work and to seek help for my damaged soul through Sonrise Family Ministry (http://www.sonrise.org.au/). Through their service, I felt released from the shock of knowing that I had cancer and the surgical trauma that my body went through. Consequently, in the September 2010, I went through another session to deal with some hidden issues. It is amazing to see how God works through this ministry, and to know that God is gracious and gentle, dealing with hurt and painful issues *only* when we are ready to allow Him to do so. Because I was ready, I experienced another extra doze of freedom.

Fun Activities in Melbourne

I started to sort out some of my belongings; some of it to bless others, and some to bring back with me by maximising the airline's acceptable luggage weight of 30kg. Five weeks was not enough to do all these because there was so much that I loved to do in Melbourne. Some of the fun things that we did as a group, included making some yummy food, like those in the pictures below.

Home-made moon cake — lotus paste with a salted egg yolk.

Siao Long Pow (mini bun)

I hang out a lot with my "friends", and would definitely miss them. I would miss admiring them and even "talking" to them. Yes, you guessed it...I mean the flowers in my garden! God's creation! "I will miss the lovely colours, the different shapes, sizes and uniqueness on each of you." Below are some of my "friends". They always brightened my day, especially, when I was down and discouraged. They were there to continually remind me that there is a God who cares for all His creation, even my "friends" below. How much *more* will He care for me?

Aren't they lovely? I will miss the blooming of this flower.

Below was taken from an ecard by Dayspring that I received:

He Is With You

*You are a fighter, a survivor, a woman of faith. You are a
tough opponent for any challenge. Even the big "C" is no
match for you because you belong to an even bigger "C"...
Christ. He is with you and many prayers are for you as
you fight this battle. You answer me and encourage me by
giving me the strength I need.*

(Psalm 138:3 TLB)

Wow! The big "C" is actually smaller than the bigger "C" who is
Christ, my Lord! I had not thought of the word big "C" and small "c".
I just loved it! What an encouragement.

CHAPTER 15

Take Two!

It was time again for me to have a CT scan on 5th October 2010 and I choose to believe that the scan result would be good. On 12th October 2010, I went to see the oncologist to get the result of the CT scan.

I wished I could write here that the result showed what I chose to believe as all clear and normal. But, the truth was not. There was one nodule in the right lower lobe of my lungs which had grown from 4mm in January 2010 to 9mm in October. This was not removed because it was too small to pluck it out during the March surgery. I needed to have another CT scan on 30th November 2010 and a follow-up review on 7th December 2010. By that time, I would be advised to consult the surgeon (if it grew bigger again) to have it removed or to use laser treatment.

Disappointment!

Needless to say, I was very disappointed. As in the past, I needed time to process what I heard from the consultation room. I felt overwhelmed at the oncologist room. I walked in that room full of confidence. I even asked the oncologist whether he was giving me good news. When he told me, "It depends on how you see it", my heart sunk. I knew my expectation was dashed.

I felt like I was inching close to the peak of the mountain and I had just lost my grip to a downward plunge. I also felt that I lost my focus and I was not hanging on tight enough. I needed some time to process or to catch my breath before I could start climbing up that slippery slope of the mountain again.

If I were not a believer in Christ, I would have felt that my life was meaningless and I would not even have that "glimpse of hope" that kept me *on* and up from the base *of* "the mountain". I still trusted Him. I knew He would carry me through and I would reach the summit in victory – one day.

At that juncture, I could still thank God because they did not find any new nodules. I thanked Him for being there with me to receive the news. I thanked Him for each bonus day and for each part of my body. I thanked Him for all of my friends and much more. I still clung on to Him and I prayed for a miracle. As my encouragement for that day:

> *"Difficulty is the very atmosphere of miracles – it is a miracle in its first stage. If it is to be a great miracle, the condition is not difficulty but impossibility. The clinging hand of His child makes a desperate situation a delight to Him."*
>
> (from "Streams in the Desert," 14th October)

Besides being disappointed and discouraged with the result, I was disappointed that I still faced an uncertain future. I also felt demoralised when I tried looking for a part-time job that would allow me some flexible time off for medical appointments or even medical leave if I needed surgery. I was not offered any job. But I still knew that He knows my heart and He has plans for me. All I needed was time out with Him to come to terms with all these disappointments and have peace.

October

October 2008 turned my world upside down. October 2010 brought disappointments. What could I say? Am I out of the woods? Or am I still at the valley? Could I ask: "Daddy, am I there, yet?"

I wanted desperately to believe that I was very near to the mountain top. Although I had slipped two steps backward, I did make a step forward, and therefore, I felt I was getting there.

To my "Cheer Team"

Friends, keep cheering me up, I have not given up. At times, I just needed the space to grasp the extra breath.

I know all of your concerns, and I know all of you love me. It had been two tough years, and it was a decision that I made in October 2008 to persevere regardless of the unpleasant journey.

Hopelessness has never been my thought, but helplessness had been in my thoughts these two years. I had Faith in Him and He brought me Hope. Basically, He was and He is still my HOPE! I felt helpless, to be caught in the uncertainties. What else could I say, except that I downloaded lots of things to Him? I learnt to allow my mind to grieve with the disappointment and to release my emotional condition to Him. I am still learning to move on to the next phase of my journey.

November

November was dreaded. On 23rd November 2010, I needed to have a colonoscopy and another CT scan on 30th November 2010. I detested drinking that yucky drink which caused tummy upset and toilet runs. This was a required procedure, as it helped to clear everything inside the intestine, so that during the colonoscopy, the colon could be clearly seen.

Feeling bored, I signed up for Prayer Ministry Skills (PMS) course run by Ellel Ministries (http://www.ellelministries.org/singapore). It was scheduled on 13th November 2010 for five Saturdays from 9:00 a.m. to 5:30 p.m. Since I had done a similar course half way through in Melbourne and stopped because of my health, I was glad that I could do it with Ellel Ministries in Singapore.

In my Thoughts

It was about twenty seven months since I fell into this valley. It had been rough and tough journey. How did my "cheer team" up there feel? When I fell, were you all discouraged? Did you all feel tired of cheering and just feel like pulling me out of the valley (which may be easier), than see me slip down yet again? There were many more questions.

I did not cope very well in November; especially when I had the colonoscopy. I was told briefly that they found a polyp during the procedure and had taken a sample for biopsy. That shocked me. Those words fell hard on me.

God knew before hand. He had prepared a way for me. After attending the Prayer Ministry Skills course by Ellel Ministries, I found out that they have a retreat house, where one could sign up and go for two nights and two days, to spend time with God, and have ministry time. I signed up for that, and the course happened to fall on the evening of the day of my colonoscopy on 23rd November.

At first, I thought it might be too rush for me to go there in the evening, after having a procedure in the late morning. I still went.

I was clueless as to what I have signed for. I was unaware that they had a programme in this time out with God. But no regrets! I was thankful that I went!

The extract below encouraged me whenever I was at the waiting room at National Cancer Centre. This is quoted by Amy Givler in her book, *"Hope in the Face of Cancer"*.

"For cancer is so limited –
It cannot cripple love,
It cannot shatter hope,
It cannot corrode faith,
It cannot destroy peace,
It cannot kill friendship,
It cannot suppress memories,
It cannot silence courage,
It cannot invade the soul,
It cannot steal God's gift of eternal life,
It cannot quench the Holy Spirit,
It cannot lessen the power of the resurrection."

(Author Unknown)

View of the moon from the bedroom, when I could not sleep.

Heading for Colonoscopy and Retreat

After the colonoscopy, Lena, my sister-in-Christ who went with me to the hospital, brought me out for lunch and then sent me home. Thanks Lena! Still feeling sleepy from the anaesthesia, I went to sleep for about an hour, woke up, and got myself ready to go for the retreat with God. All excited about it, I left the house about 5:00 p.m., took the shuttle bus to the interchange, and went to buy insect repellent because it was in an area with many mosquitoes. I then hopped on the MRT to Paya Lebar East/West Line where I could change my route in the Circle Line to Marymount. I arrived at the Paya Lebar interchange at the start of the peak hour at 6:00 p.m. and managed to get into the crowded Circle Line. After a few stops, seeing people coming in and out of the train, I heard the train's-speaker system announcing that the next stop would be at Paya Lebar. I was shocked and surprised. "Didn't I start with the Circle Line from Paya Lebar? How come my next stop is Paya Lebar?" I came out of the train, back to the station and looked around. It *was* Paya Lebar station! So, I hopped back onto the correct train and went back toward Marymount station (At this point of writing, the circle line, started from Paya Lebar and ended at Marymount station).

My brain had shut down. I was dazed even though I did not sleep during the travel. The train took me round that circle again (I've proven that it *is* a circle line!). I arrived at my designated station 54 minutes later! That should have taken a mere 18 minutes from the Paya Lebar station. Arggghhh!

I was late and I still needed to walk about 10 minutes to the retreat house. Since I was clueless about the venue, I decided to take a taxi. I gave the driver the address and said it was somewhere ahead, not knowing that he did not know the place either! He drove me to a dead end road with no houses. Thankfully, God knew. One of the ministry team members from the retreat house called me on my mobile to find out what happened to me and gave instructions to the driver. Isn't our God great? His perfect timing!

More Surprises

After settling down, I was introduced to the ministry teams and six participants. Each of us had a counsellor and a co-counsellor. That evening, I had an introduction time with the counsellor and co-counsellor before our rest. The next few days were spent having devotion time, meals, ministry and counselling time, time with God, and fellowship.

When I signed up for the retreat, I did not know counsellors were there to walk us through our issues. God had been walking this journey with me. He knew what I needed and He opened all doors for me at the perfect time. The counsellor and the co-counsellor who walked with me had been very encouraging. They helped me to continue up the slope and to reach the mountain top. I remain eternally thankful to both of them for their help and encouragement.

Next – Results.

7th December 2010, was the day for the review of the CT scan and colonoscopy. That day, I went to the oncologist with lots of "ifs", "*what if...?*" Fear and uncertainties crept in, whilst waiting for my turn. It seemed like I was waiting for ages though there fewer patients than usual. Finally, I walked into the familiar room, sat on the same chair and exchanged greetings. I heard the "final verdict":

Oncologist : *"your result showed* **no new cancer cells and the one that was there is still the same size at 9mm.**"

Me : *"Wow! But hang on. What are you going to do with that one?"*

Oncologist : *"Nothing! Just see me again in 3 or 4 months time. Now I need to listen to your breathing and..."*

Me : *"You mean I don't need to see Dr. A, and you are not cutting me up again? So, I* ***only come back in 4 months' time?"***

Oncologist : *"Yes that's right. You must be praying
very hard, right?"*

Me : *"Of course, not only me but my cheer
team and all my loved ones. He is faithful!
Thanks for this report. It was the best
that you had given to me, and my best
Christmas present."*

After I settled the next appointment for x-ray and review which would
be in April 2011, I went back home to have time with Him before
heading for the next appointment in the late afternoon.

This was a different eagle;
I could see it was brownish in colour when it soared nearer to my window.
I captured this photograph as I was spending time with Him in the afternoon.

I arrived around 2:45 p.m. at Changi General Hospital. After all the
necessary registration and paper work was completed, I waited for
my turn. It was a long wait! I only got to see Dr. W at about 4:00
p.m. With a good and favourable result in the morning, I was more
confident now, but not sure what the biopsy would show. I was told
by Dr. W that the biopsy showed up **benign** and that the polyp was

a hyperplasic type. In simple terms, it would not develop into cancer cells. So, they **would not do anything to it** but will do another colonoscopy in one year's time, which would be end of 2011.

Big Thanks

Thanks to all of my "cheer team" for praying, walking alongside with me and most of all, I want to thank Abba Father! Thanks for His Healing Hands, for His Grace, and for being there when I fell. Thanks for bringing the right people at the right time, in my moment of need. Thanks for granting my Christmas wish.

One of my favourite songs by Don Moen, "*Like Eagles*":

> "…………..
> …………
>
> *O my soul, don't be afraid*
> *Hope in the Lord*
> *By His righteousness and power*
> *He will strengthen, He will guide*
>
> *And I will soar on wings like eagles*
> ……….
> ……….
> *For the Lord is never weary*
> ……………………
> ……………………"
>
> (Isaiah 40:28-31)

CHAPTER 16

Time for Reflection!

At the end of 2010, I felt it was time for me to do some "auditing" of my life. Since October 2008, I had been on a long and tedious journey to a yet to be revealed destination. I was in a roller coaster ride, going up and down with such speed, that I was not given any time to prepare for. It was a whirlwind of tests, scans, reviews, chemo, surgery, and other bad news. It came without a warning, and I was in it for almost 27 months. Time flew. In those 27 months, I had to learn to cope with reverse culture shock, the illusive dreams, the physical pain, the emotional pendulum, the sense of helplessness, and even more. It was not easy but I am thankful that I had God. Below is an extract from "*Streams in the Desert*," 13th December:

> "*If you are in the deep shadows because of some strange, mysterious providence, do not be afraid. Simply go on in faith and love, never doubting. God is watching, and He will bring good and beauty out of all your pain and tears.*"
>
> (J.R. Miller)

God is good. He had never forsaken me. He has been real to me throughout this journey. He even entertained me with His creation: the eagles, the stars, the seas and all the greenery. He is just awesome!

He knew how much I could take. When I was at the breaking point, He sent people around me, to encourage me, walk with me and prayed with me – all in the nick of time.

Plans for Closure in Melbourne

My next trip to Melbourne would be time for me to do some closure. I had to do more packing of books and clothing and arranged to send them back to Singapore. I booked the flight to Melbourne on 9th January 2011 and stayed there close to three months before returning back to Singapore for my follow-up medical review around April. I was still unsure of what I would be doing but trusted that He would direct me to His master plan.

I spent my time sleeping, reading, and enjoying my "special friends" in the garden. What a good reminder to know that despite minimal care from my dear daughter, my Heavenly Dad had taken great care of them all. He brought them enough rain when N forgot to water them and they survived and grew very well. Similarly, there were times I was too caught up with worldly matters that I forgot I have a God who provides for all my needs as written in Matthew 6:25-33.

Spending time with His creation and with nature, be it in the garden or at the windows admiring how the eagles soar freely in the sky – always gave me that nudge to refocus on Him. It reminded me of His cares for each one of us.

N and I managed to have a weekend away at W. Gippsland, exploring His creation at the waterfalls and surrounding scenery.

"No person who allows his mind to be ruled by his senses can have victorious faith. The mind that is ruled by the senses lives in a realm of uncertainty."
("Christ the Healer," by F.F. Bosworth)

"I am not alone in this journey
Dad you are with me
When I was bored

Birds chip along
Breeze blew into my face
Ships, barges cruise by

I am not alone in this journey
Dad you are with me
When I was discouraged

Eagles soar in the sky
Encouraging words flood in
Emails, phones all seems working

I am not alone in this journey
Dad you are with me
When I was at breaking point

You pick me up
Send people around me
To love, encourage, and walk with me.

Thanks my Dad
You are the Faithful, Trustworthy
And You are my ALL!"
(written on 21st December 2010)

Moving House

I started packing some of my things to bring back to Singapore. I ended up packing almost the whole house! The rental fees of that unit was set to increase and N thought to downsize, would help her to save cost since I would not be in Melbourne often. We found a unit.

We picked up the keys of the new unit on Thursday evening. We were grateful that the unit had been well cleaned and well kept. Friday was busy. We managed to borrow a vehicle from Operation Mobilization (OM) to move the boxes that we had packed in the last couple of days. Thanks to Eric and Jik for helping out and Lianna for all the boxes. The mover came on Saturday morning of the 26th March to move all the big items from the old unit. N and I spend the rest of the day unpacking and, by evening, we returned the vehicle. On Sunday and Monday, we spent our time cleaning up the other unit, had the carpet shampooed, and did more unpacking at the new place. Tuesday, we went back to the old unit to hand over the keys and say good-bye to the unit that we called home for six years. That was the closure of a season in my life filled with fond memories.

Laptop

My laptop was "ill" during my time in Melbourne, it was so "sick" that I had to admit it to the "hospital". It stayed with Toshiba agent from 3rd March to 29th March. It played up on my first day in Melbourne, but I managed to get help, and it was revived but soon, it gave me problems again. I decided to send it to Toshiba for repair, since it was still under warranty and, thankfully, all within the right timing. It was a hard drive issue and unknown to me, the web camera was not functioning fully which explained why it took them so long to fix it. I am thankful that it happened just before the warranty expired. I concluded that even equipment can fall "ill" sometimes and need time out for recovery!

Journey Back to Singapore

I arrived in Singapore on Sunday midnight, 4th April and had to be at the National Cancer Centre in the late morning to have an x-ray. The follow-up review would be on Friday, 8th April 2011. The x-ray report was good – no trace of the cancer cells. The cancer cells either had not grown any bigger or had shrunk or even left my body. The oncologist was happy to do the next review until close to six months later. The next CT scan was set for September, followed by review a week later.

I chose to believe that He had healed me as I felt physically great and my digestive system had been behaving well. Thanks to Him. Thanks to all my friends for praying.

Discovery

During the time of packing and cleaning the units in Melbourne, I found that the numbness in my hands and feet from the chemo were still in my system even if it had been two years since the chemotherapy treatment ended. I needed to be careful, make some adjustments and "may have to learn to live with it" (quote from the oncologist).

Please stand alongside with me to pray that I need not "live with it", that someday, He will reverse this side effect back to normal.

Work

I was back in Singapore, adjusting to the hot and humid weather. I was caught in a storm twice, once on my way to the dentist, and the second, on my way to work.

Yes! I started a half-day job. I was recommended a job on my return to Singapore. When I went for the interview, I told them that I would only work for four hours a day to help me adjust back to working, since I had not been able to work for more than two and a half years.

I started work on 12th April. The first week was a struggle. I had not been working in Singapore for a long time. I needed to adapt to the fast pace, no breaks, long-working hours culture. I had to review my language capabilities in speaking dialects and try to re-learn reading the Chinese characters that I had not used for eons. The travelling time on public transport was a contrast to the leisurely walk to work in Melbourne, where I could enjoy and admire His creation. I could not seem to keep to the four hours of work daily without doing additional hours.

I left the job at the end of May, finding it too stressful. I needed my space and time back again. It did not work out as I expected. I spent lots of time catching up with lost sleep in the first week of June after I stopped working. I did not realise that the one and a half months of work took its toil on me.

I was recalled to work in the same company again, as they intended to wind up the business and wanted the accounts to be finalised. I agreed to go back as a full-time staff on 16th June to finish the May and first half of June's accounts before deciding to switch to part-time work or to quit. So, there I was, back to work again. No more sleeping in. No more afternoon naps. No more looking out for the eagles.

Little Sarah and Me

There were days when I would go over to B's place to play with my new "playmate" – none other than my grand-daughter Sarah. She was growing fast, and was fun to play with. However, she woke up frequently and played up at night on her parents. That's why she needed grandma to be her playmate while mum took a zzzzzzz. She turned one in June.

In Between Time

Since I started work soon after I returned from Melbourne, I found that I had very little time to do the things I did during the last two years. For once, I found those times where I had nothing to do very precious. Those were the time where I could sit and admire the eagles, see the passing ships and aeroplanes. Suddenly, I had to squeeze into packed trains and see the other side of His creation – mostly the different and unique individuals that He created. What a contrast!

I filled this gap of waiting for the next CT scan and colonoscopy with part time work, my "playmate", Sarah and writing this book. Time just raced by.

Outing

In more recent times, I had been out to the Orchard Road area, met friends after work and attended a seminar conducted by Rev William Lau from Texas, who has been involved in the healing ministries with the Elijah Challenge (http://revalbertkang.tripod.com/ebulletin/id9.html). I felt like an alien in my own country when the buildings and landmarks I was accustomed to were no more and new buildings had replaced them.

The biggest surprised was our National Library. It used to be a red-brick building. The National Library has moved to another site with new-modern structure. Oh! It is not only *human* "life" that has its season, but it seems everything, even buildings have seasons, too! I learnt to treasure every season, be blessed by every moment that God had given, and live life to its fullest.

Discouraging

It was another challenging waiting game. As I waited for the next medical review, not knowing what to expect, but trusting that He is ever in control. I prayed that the end of the tunnel would be near. I did not understand why I had cancer, but I know that in this journey, He brought people with cancer into my path. Being a cancer patient myself, I understood and I was able to relate to the journey most of them were going through. There was some discouraging news along the way. One case was that of a relative of ours, who lost their 37 year old son to brain cancer. It pained my heart to know, that he left behind two young children. Another friend had a relapse and, subsequently, discovered that her sister *also* had cancer. There were a few more friends who were not doing that well, either. It was so heart-breaking to hear and see all these happenings in this fallen world. I was discouraged. I also felt that my life had been on a standstill for "ages". I was not out of the wood and the future remained uncertain. How could I assist in this area? I am to encourage and not to discourage people (and of course, readers).

Medical Review

I had my CT scan on 16th September 2011 and the colonoscopy on Tuesday, 20th September. The review for both the results would be available on Friday, 23rd September.

I was at the National Cancer Centre in the morning and I saw the oncologist. The CT scan result was yet another disappointment. I was given an appointment to consult the surgeon on Tuesday, 27th September. The report showed that the cancer cells in the right lung had grown to more than 1cm. I was disillusioned to hear and see the report. They had found a confirmed cancer cell cluster in the left lung which was also over 1cm and two suspicious-looking small spots.

With total disillusionment and uncertainty about the next phase, I left to visit a friend who was an in-patient at the hospital. She was recovering from surgery about a week prior. She, too, has cancer. We prayed that with this surgery, she could recover and have a new lease of life. I left for Changi General Hospital to receive the report for the colonoscopy. At least, I had a positive result for this. I returned home and cried my heart out. I believed God heard me and He was collecting all my tear drops as He promised in His Word. I needed to wait until Tuesday to know what the lung surgeon would suggest and what he wanted to do. I had three days to grieve and to come to terms with the CT scan result.

Tuesday, 27th September 2011, was a bad beginning. It started at 3:00 a.m. when I was woken by discomfort in my stomach. I rushed to the toilet, vomited, and this was followed by a bout of diarrhoea. After three to four times of vomiting, it stopped, but the diarrhoea continued on until the next day. By late morning, I was completely worn out that I could only run to the toilet and to fall flat on the bed. Around noon, I managed to pull myself out of bed, get dressed and took a taxi to the hospital for the appointment with the lung surgeon. Thankfully, I managed to travel for about 40 minutes. Once I arrived at the hospital, the first thing I did was to rush to the toilet.

After the registration for the appointment, I was given a queue number and, again, I waited for my turn. In the consultation room, the surgeon presented my medical report and suggested that I needed *another* surgery. The cancer cell, that was on the right lower lobe of my lung, had grown bigger and attached to one of "the bronchial trees" (the blood vessels to the lungs). He needed to tie that blood vessel up to stop it from bleeding, which would stop the supply of the blood to the remainder of the lower lobe of the right lung. In that situation, it would be better to remove the whole lower lobe of the right lung. In the scan, it also showed that the left lower lobe of the lung had one cancer cell that was almost the same size as the right lung. There were two to three other smaller ones. The next suggestion was to remove the left lower lobe, too. Then, I would be surviving without the two lower lobes of the lungs. Initially, I would not have enough stamina, until I slowly build up the capacity within my remaining lungs. He suggested a surgery in October.

After throwing many questions at the surgeon, I decided to push the surgery to four months later and arranged for a CT scan at the end of January 2012, followed by review on 7th February 2012. By then we would have decided the date for surgery. In the meantime, I wanted to make full use of those four months to do what I may not be able to do in future. Most of all, I needed my time out with Him, to seek His comfort, peace and presence.

CHAPTER 17

In the Meantime...

On 5th October, Lena and I flew to Port Klang, Malaysia and spent four nights on Logos Hope. It was a memorable experience to be on board, and to meet some old friends. I am thankful to Gwen for taking us to Petaling Jaya for a day trip fellowship. About a week later, N came back for a stop-over before heading to Nepal for couple of months. I was excited to see her, but at the same time, I was concerned about her safety.

I was encouraged and felt lifted up when I went for a follow-up counselling. When I read *"I will uphold you with my righteous right hand"*, I was assured again that I was not travelling on the bumpy journey alone. One day, I saw an eaglet soaring in the sky and it lost its balance, almost falling down. However, it managed to flap its wings and it started to soar again. It reminded me that when I fell down, God was always there to lift me up. *Psalm* 121:1-2 says:

> *"....where does my help comes from? My help comes from the Lord..."*

I left on 1st November 2011 for Melbourne to housesit and have fellowship time with friends. Eric and Sandra fetched me from the airport and we had a nice *cuppa* before they sent me home. I am thankful to God that in the midst of disappointment over my health, He taught me to be appreciative of things that I used to take for granted, like relaxing on a *cuppa* with good friends.

The next couple of days, I spent most of my time with my "special friends" – my plants and giving them the extra TLC. On one of the weekends, I went with four other friends to climb the Thousand Steps in Mount Dandenong, Victoria. It was an achievement to be able to reach the summit although I met a climber who made two rounds and I struggled just with one.

Tired but finally at the top of thousand steps

One of the Sunday speakers at church, Mark Conner spoke about the "Stages of Faith" — Recognition of God, Life of Discipleship, Productive Life, Journey Inward, Journey Outward and Life of Love. It truly spoke to me. My trials of the last three years, gave me the confidence and assurance of my recognition of who God is and how powerful He is. Without FAITH, I would have lost all HOPE, not even to publish this book. I thought, "Did I keep looking at my disappointment and forget all the blessings that had come from Him? How often did I take things for granted and only focussed on my disappointment?" Even in the worst situation or disappointment, I could still find things to be thankful for.

Oh yes! I even had a pre-Christmas shopping spree where I shopped till I dropped at 4:00 a.m.! What's more? I went for a week's trip with friends to Sydney, returning only on 4th January 2012. It was a relaxing and memorable trip, although I started to have a bad sore throat and cough. I also missed one of those toilet runs when I needed to queue for my turn and, consequently, got messed up. I still managed to make the best out of the worst situation and enjoyed my trip. I also had time out with N upon her return to Geelong, Portarlington and the "Fairy Park". It was amazing to learn the history of the place and how a dream came true in 1956. After all the fun and catching up with friends, it was time to pack up and head back to Singapore on 29th January 2012 for a CT scan two days later.

Back in Singapore

I went for my CT scan and waited for a week for my review. In the meantime, B was expecting her second child and she was showing signs that the baby might arrive early. I spent some nights at their house when she was having false contractions and needed to be in hospital. My review for the CT scan was set for the 7th February. Thankfully, Fiona was with me to give me the moral support. The result was not in my favour. The surgeon, Dr. K, decided that I should have the surgery as soon as possible as I had delayed it for almost four months. I asked Dr. K to schedule the surgery six to eight weeks later, so that by then my second grandchild would have arrived. He was not comfortable with the decision but he agreed to it. In the meantime, the date for the lung function test and surgery was arranged.

At that time, I wished that my loved ones could be more understanding about my emotions. I had to deal with disappointments at the prospect of a third invasive surgery, where the surgeon would remove the lower lobe of both lungs. Although, I knew that my adult children's lives were in control and organized, knowing that the false alarm of the arrival of the second grandchild caused some adjustments in the family. Being a mum, I wanted so much to be there for them and not to be a burden to them. Maybe all mothers would have the same concern and do the same. Hence, I chose to delay the surgery and trust that God would continue to protect and keep me safe.

I had my lung function test on the 15th February and was thankful it was a quick process. My review with Dr. K and Dr. T was 21st February. The surgery was fixed on 26th March 2012.

Exciting News

My second grandchild was born on 25th February. I thank God that I had the chance to see this new addition and to be able to carry him. The next couple of weeks, my time were divided between the grandchildren, my own home, and medical appointment where I had a routine review with Dr. W.

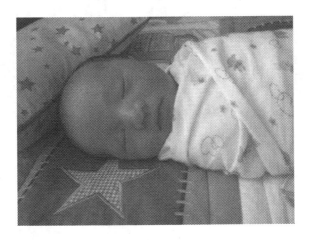

Ewan DOB 25.02.12

I had an interesting experience at Kingdom Invasion 2012. Bill Johnson was the speaker that night and he spoke about Faith and Believe. When he started to pray, and F who was with me, prayed as well, I felt God's presence and His peace. It was an unexplainable awesome experience of some heat around my lungs area, and tingling around my foot. At the same time, I saw some red flashes of light in front of me. I did not understand what was going on in my body but I trusted that He would heal me in His timing.

Third Surgery

I needed to do a pre-operation test on the 19th March. I checked in at the "7 Stars Hotel" named Singapore General Hospital, a week later. The following morning was the surgery and I was the first patient. The nurses got me ready by seven in the morning. Soon, I was in the operating theatre and the anaesthetist came to explain the procedure and suggested using epidural to control the pain after the general anaesthesia wore off. Once I agreed and signed the necessary documentation, he inserted the needles at the back of my spine and I soon drifted into deep slumber.

When they woke me up and told me all was over, I was in terrible pain, especially my right shoulder. I was semi-conscious and knew that I was at the recovery room for a long time, as they were trying to adjust the epidural to control the pain. When I was settled with the pain, they sent me to the High Dependency (HD) Ward. N came to visit me but I could not remember much except the pain. It hurt and the only position I could lay was flat on my back. I could not move with all the tubes around. Every move I made, hurt. Due to the medication, I slept most of the time. Being in the HD ward, I lost track of day or night. The nurses were constantly checking on me that I hardly had a peaceful rest. The pain was unbearable, and I remembered calling to God to help me be able to sleep. I felt much better the next couple of days, but I still had the epidural and needed to be in the HD for another night.

I started with soft diet and used the bed pan in the HD even for "big business". Finally, on the fourth day, after they removed the epidural, I was allowed to move to the general ward. It was good to be back in the same ward I was admitted to. My bed was at the window area which was good for viewing but not for diarrhoea, as it meant a longer walk to the toilet. I was not comfortable asking for a bed pan and nurses in the general ward had more patients to handle. I was looking forward to going home the next day. But the bad diarrhoea recurred. I could not run. I could only try to walk as fast as I could which did not help. On top of that I had to carry the drainage box which was attached with a tube at the side of my chest. I did mess up and needed the nurses' help. Thank God, they moved me closer to the entrance which helped tremendously. I now had a shorter distance to walk. Due to the diarrhoea, my potassium level dropped to only 2.9 and I needed to have a potassium drip. It was burning hot at the vein. So, they changed sites and gave me ice pack to place on it, which helped. It was Sunday, and I was hoping that I could be discharged to attend church. I felt much better, and my appetite returned, too. Dr. K came to do the rounds on Monday morning and told me that I could be discharged. That was good news! N came to the hospital at 11:00 a.m. and we waited for the medication. I arranged with my brother to drive us home at 12:30 p.m. We finally left the hospital, and on our way back, stopped to buy lunch. Arriving home, I had lunch and went to bed. I had a good rest with no nurses coming to take blood pressure (BP) or temperature. N was preparing to bake cookies and our dinner. I spent eight nights in the hospital and being home to sleep on my own bed, made a world of difference.

Re-Admitted

The next day, my abdomen area hurt badly, so I took painkiller and went to bed. At midnight the pain was excruciating that I had to struggle to get out of bed to take more painkiller, before snuggling back to bed. I was expecting Ps J and SM to visit me late in the morning. After breakfast, I was relaxing, listening to music and the abdominal pain started again. The painkiller did not help. When Ps J and SM came, I was vomiting. SM sent me to hospital and I was re-admitted to Changi General Hospital in the afternoon for six nights. Upon arrival, I was given Pethidine. What a relief! The x-ray result showed that I had an obstruction in my intestine. They gave me drips and fleet. The fleet helped to clear off the blockage, but the pain remained. I only managed to sleep for about three hours because

I was woken up by one of the room-mates who was groaning away. I was home for merely two nights to sleep in my own bed and was back to the hospital again.

The obstruction could be the result of ingesting the painkiller and the diarrhoea medication. I was given another round of fleet but I still felt nausea. I was not prepared for this stay in the hospital. I did not have any books to read. Although I was bored, it gave me the time to learn to be still and to listen to God's voice. On the second day, I vomited and messed up the bed. The nurse came and inserted a tube through my nose and took out another 120 ml of liquid. Thankfully, I felt much better by nightfall.

The third day, I still had the nasal tube on. It was uncomfortable. I was praying that they could remove it quickly. Finally, my tummy was more settled and feeling much better. This time, I began to feel the surgical pain around my lungs area. They transferred me to the same room and bed of my first admission. I remembered counting the aeroplanes! Wow, it was almost four years since the beginning of my journey. I wondered, "Am I out of the woods?"

Another day went by, and the nasal tube was removed. It was a relief and my throat felt so much better. I was allowed to have some clear liquid feed of up to 1 litre. Unfortunately, I started to have diarrhoea and the medical team decided to do a thorough test, even a stool test. I was always waking up at around 2:00 a.m. and was unable to get back to sleep. The next day, the diarrhoea was less frequent. A few visitors came. My diet was changed to Low Residual Diet. After many days without food, it really tasted yummy!

It was Easter Sunday and I was reflecting on my arduous cancer journey – three surgeries, six cycles of chemotherapy and two obstruction admissions. I realised that even with the general anaesthesia (GA), morphine and painkiller, I still complained about the immense pain. The pain was hard to cope. My thoughts went to Golgotha where Jesus was crucified. He did not have any GA, morphine or painkiller. The excruciating pain He endured must have been many times worse than mine, yet, He died not for His own sins but for mine. He took my pain on the cross!

Finally, on Tuesday, 10th April 2012, I was discharged from hospital. I was home by afternoon. It was awesome to be home and to have uninterrupted sleep in the night. I slept well that night. My body learnt to cope with two third lungs on both sides. With His grace, the pain, energy and strength improved each day as *Isaiah* 41:10 says,

"...I will strengthen you and help you.."

I had a medical review with Dr. W, a follow-up after my discharged from the hospital. Four days later, I had review with my oncologist. I was glad to hear that my next x-ray and review would be six months later, in November. This was the longest gap that I had.

I flew to Melbourne on 1st June for my RRR (Rest, Restore and Rejoice) and I stayed until 4th August. I had a great time of rest, catching up with friends and gobbling all the yummy food and coffee that I dearly missed.

Medical Review

I had an x-ray and medical review with Dr. K on 7th August 2012 and the result was satisfactory. At the end of August, I had medical review with Dr. W. He mentioned the existence of a nodule that was not clearly shown on the x-ray which I was not told of earlier. I was surprised, shocked and disappointed. Next, I had a colonoscopy on 20th November. As usual on the eve of the colonoscopy day, I needed to fast and take the oral fleet to clear all the waste in the system. I was in the hospital by eight in the morning and was all done and ready to go home about six hours later. Esther came and we went for lunch before sending me home. Nine days later, I went for my chest x-ray at the National Cancer Centre. A week later, I had my review. Since Dr. T was on leave, I saw his assistant. I was told that the x-ray report showed that the nodule was stable but they were unsure what it was. So, I went for a CT scan on

15ᵗʰ December. It was very discouraging, but I still trusted that in His time, God would completely heal me. The CT scan did not take long. I had learnt to relax and to trust God for whatever the outcome of the result. It was pointless to be anxious. Dr. T's assistant gave me the impression that he was inexperienced. He tried his best to relate the report to me. It didn't sound promising. They found a "balloon" in the right lung. So, he arranged to bring forward my appointment with my surgeon, Dr. K to 29ᵗʰ January 2013. I was told that I was a "high risk" patient.

What news to receive with Christmas just round the corner! I was shattered. Although I knew I was once a Stage 4 colorectal cancer patient, there was no need to slap me with a "high risk" patient label. An encouragement to live life to the fullest was a good enough. I asked myself, "What happened to my faith?" I chose to response to God's promises in His book with Faith. My Faith helped me to Trust God. I always said I will live life to its fullest for each day, because I am unsure when will be my last. Luci Swindoll wrote:

> *"Each person has a spiritual obligation before God to learn how to live well, to live fully, as opposed to knowing only how to live comfortably."*

I was down with a bad cough the next couple of days. I believed I must have picked up the virus from the hospital. Although I had not fully recovered from the cough, I flew with B's family to Bangkok on Christmas Day. We had four days of eating yummy food.

On 15ᵗʰ March 2013, I went to the National Cancer Centre for my review. It was a long agonizing wait. When I got into the consultation room, Dr. T told me that the scan was all clear – no new cancerous cells found.

I was *cancer free*!

Wow, the word "cancer free" sounded like a magic word. I started to question about the "nodule" on my left lung, and also the "balloon" on the right lung? The "nodule" on the left lung, turned out to be scar tissue. The "balloon" on the right lung was due to post-op fluid, which would drain off in time.

I was lost for words. All I could say was, "Thank You, God." All Praise to Him. This was the best news that I had waited for four years and five months to hear. It finally came. I was the most grateful, most excited, most overwhelmed and most overjoyed person!

I am God's miracle!

What's next? I am off to United State to visit some friends before the next follow-up at the end of 2013.

Conclusion

Thankful that I could spend time seeing my granddaughter, Sarah and enjoying her!

O n 17th August 2011, I was having lunch with one of my pastors, and she reminded me of these bible verses:

*"**One thing** I ask of the Lord, this is what I seek; that I may **dwell** in the house of the Lord **all the days of my life**, **to gaze** upon the **beauty of the Lord** and **seek him** in **his temple**."*

(Psalm 27:4 NIV)

"For I know the plans I have for you," declares the Lord, "plans to prosper you and not to harm you, plans to give you hope and a future."

(Jeremiah 29:11 NIV)

I asked myself, "How am I going to make the best out of my cancer journey? What legacy do I want to leave for my loved ones, friends and all to remember? In which area could I still serve Him and be able to contribute to people that He brings along my path, and to the community? Am I still qualified to do God's work?"

God does not call the qualified, but He qualifies the CALLED. Let's look at some of the big names in the Bible: Jacob was a cheater, Peter had a temper, David had an affair, Noah got drunk, Jonah ran away from God, Paul and Moses were murderers, Gideon, Miriam, Martha, Thomas, Sara, Elijah, and many others. With all these, I felt that I was just as qualified as them and I would let God use me in the bonus days, months, and years that He is going to bless me with, to bless others.

This book chronicles my cancer journey replete with the honest emotions and struggles I had. I pray that with my openness in sharing my emotional roller coaster, and my moving three steps forwards and sliding two steps backwards, would serve as an encouragement to people who are in a similar journey and, who are finding it hard to cope. I hope that this book will help you to understand the emotional journey of those who are in a similar situation. Is it normal to feel uncertain, hopeless, and helpless? Are we allowed to be discouraged and disappointed? Can we over-react? How do you come to terms with the whole cancer diagnosis? I hope that by penning it all down, you will be encouraged.

The song below was played in church on 4th September:

> "…………
> …………
> *There can be miracles*
> *When you believe*
> *Though hope is frail*
> …………
> …………
> …………
> *You will when you believe*
> *Just believe ……..*"
>
> (Whitney Houston, "**When You Believe**"
> From The Prince Of Egypt lyrics)

I believed!

Looking back at how far I have walked this journey, I believe I was able to tread the distance because I had a living God. At my lowest point, when life was helpless, lonely and I did not know what to expect next, God in His mysterious ways, would amaze me with friends calling at the right time and egging me on with encouraging words. He sent eagles soaring in the sky to remind me, "I love you *more* than the eagle."

I am thankful that God is my personal Saviour, my Healer, my Comforter, my Wrestler and my personal Friend. When I was in the dark tunnel, I could ask Him my "whys". He answered me gently. Although I did not always get an answer, I know He heard them all. I could download all my deepest emotions to my Friend, which, sometimes, were difficult to express to friends. I had His peace and assurance that He would walk with me and carry me, especially, when

I was too tired to do so. In spite of my many questions, I know that He has never been angry with me. He understands my situation completely, better than anyone else. 1 *Peter* 5:7 says:

> *"Cast all your anxiety on him because he cares for you."*
>
> (NIV)

The song "*I Almost Let* Go" by Kurt Carr, speaks a lot to me:

> *"I almost let go*
> *I felt like I just couldn't take life anymore*
> *My problems had me bound*
> *Depression weighed me down*
> ....
> ....
> *God kept me"*

I had waited for my final result to conclude in this book.

This is the amazing news. I am His walking testimony, His miracle! Although the journey was tough and unpredictable, He had sprinkled a few big memorable events like my daughter's wedding, my trips to Melbourne and my grandchildren's birth along the journey. He gave me all the extra bonus days to experience the joy of being a grandma. My granddaughter arrived three months after I had my key-hole surgery in June 2010. My grandson arrived one month before I had my last surgery in March 2012. He just celebrated his first birthday. I thank God for His Grace to have the opportunity to be a part of their lives and to see them grow. I am also thankful to God, that I had the energy and concentration to do some work, to put my journey into this humble book, to encourage **you,** – dear reader, who for some reasons singled out this text. Thanks to my Almighty!

A Bird's Eye View Of My Life

I love this prayer that I received through email from "*Prime Time with God to You*" on 7ᵗʰ October 2012:

"God, I have heard that you are never late, seldom early, but always on time. When I think back through the experiences of my life, I can see the truth in that statement. Thank you for always being on time. Thank you for the lessons you have taught me through waiting, through suffering, through the storms and valleys and for your faithfulness always. Thank you for the rays of sun that peaked through the clouds in the way of a praying spirit and helping hand from other Christians. Thank you for the sun that shone brightly after the storms and cloudy days, and for your son who is my sun and shield, the Lord Jesus Christ. If you had always been on my time schedule, I wouldn't have learned much in life, so I am thankful that you are always on time according to your schedule. I praise you for who you are and all you've done. May I be found worthy in your sight through the blood of the Saviour. In His name I pray, Amen."

Appendix – Prayers

In this book, I have mentioned time and again about my faith in my God. This faith carried me through. This faith is available to you.

I would like to invite you to have this faith that kept me through by asking Jesus Christ to come into your life.

If you are ready to let Him come into your heart and become your best friend, just say this prayer sincerely from your heart:

> *"Lord Jesus, I invite You to be my Saviour and Lord. I believe You are the Son of God and that You died for my sins. I also believe You were raised from the dead and now, You sit at the right hand of the Father. I ask for forgiveness for my sins. Help me to know You more each day. Thank You for being my Lord and best friend. Amen."*

If you have prayed this prayer, we rejoice with you in your decision. You now have a new relationship with Jesus. Please contact your local Christian church, so that they can help you become established in your relationship with Jesus. You have just made the most important decision of your life.

I made this decision many years back. Following Christ has been the singular motivation in my journey with cancer.